Lecture Notes
in Business Information Processing   186

Series Editors

Wil van der Aalst
Eindhoven Technical University, The Netherlands
John Mylopoulos
University of Trento, Italy
Michael Rosemann
Queensland University of Technology, Brisbane, Qld, Australia
Michael J. Shaw
University of Illinois, Urbana-Champaign, IL, USA
Clemens Szyperski
Microsoft Research, Redmond, WA, USA

Trine Hald Commisso
Jacob Nørbjerg
Jan Pries-Heje (Eds.)

Nordic Contributions in IS Research

5th Scandinavian Conference
on Information Systems, SCIS 2014
Ringsted, Denmark, August 10-13, 2014
Proceedings

 Springer

Volume Editors

Trine Hald Commisso
Roskilde University
Department of Communication, Business & IT
Roskilde, Denmark
E-mail: trinehc@ruc.dk

Jacob Nørbjerg
University of Aalborg
Department of Computer Science
Aalborg, Denmark
E-mail: jacobnor@cs.aau.dk

Jan Pries-Heje
Roskilde University
Department of Communication, Business & IT
Roskilde, Denmark
E-mail: janph@ruc.dk

ISSN 1865-1348   e-ISSN 1865-1356
ISBN 978-3-319-09545-5   e-ISBN 978-3-319-09546-2
DOI 10.1007/978-3-319-09546-2
Springer Cham Heidelberg New York Dordrecht London

Library of Congress Control Number: 2014944553

Typesetting: Camera-ready by author, data conversion by Scientific Publishing Services, Chennai, India

Printed on acid-free paper

Springer is part of Springer Science+Business Media (www.springer.com)

Preface

Designing Human Technologies

This book constitutes the proceedings of the 5th Scandinavian Conference on Information Systems (SCIS) that took place at Sørup Herregaard, Ringsted, Denmark, in August 2014. Since the start, SCIS has been co-located and co-organized with the IRIS Conference—the longest running information systems research conference in the world.

The theme for this book as well as for the conference is "Designing Human Technologies." The theme combines the interplay of people with technology—a classic theme in Scandinavian information systems research—with the growing interest within the IS research field in design and design science research (DSR).

Design as an activity is core to most applied research disciplines such as medicine, engineering, and information systems: Since the birth of computer science and information systems in the 1940s and 1950s, many have studied design. In the 1960s design of the man–machine interface was drawing interest. In the 1970s and 1980s there was a specific Scandinavian movement of designing systems together with the users. And the 1990s and 2000s just increased this focus on the users and their interaction with information technology.

For many years, a substantial number of research papers on design in relation to IT were published in the annual IRIS conference, in the *Scandinavian Journal of Information Systems*, and in the bi-annual Participatory Design (PD) conference. In the late 1990s and in the beginning of the present century the IS community at large recognized the importance of design science research. After the publication of the seminal book by Herbert Simon *Sciences of the Artificial* in 1996, papers started appearing in the best international IS Journals. And in 2006 the first DESRIST—Design Science Research Conference in IT—was held in Los Angeles.

Our hope this year by having "Designing Human Technologies" as our theme was to showcase the newest Scandinavian research as well as to draw the line back to classic Scandinavian IS design covering the last 50 years or so.

From the 22 submissions registered in the submission management system EasyChair, nine research papers were selected for inclusion in the proceedings. Of the accepted papers, four are written by authors from Danish universities, three from Norwegian universities, and two from Finnish universities. Two papers had co-authors from the USA and New Zealand.

We would like to acknowledge the contributions of the Program Committee and additional reviewers, and the support of Roskilde University, without whom this conference would not have been possible.

June 2014   Trine Hald Commisso
                                                                  Jacob Nørbjerg
                                                                  Jan Pries-Heje

Organization

Conference Chairs

Jacob Nørbjerg   University of Aalborg, Denmark
Jan Pries-Heje   Roskilde University, Denmark

Program Chairs

Trine Hald Commisso   Roskilde University, Denmark
Jacob Nørbjerg   University of Aalborg, Denmark
Jan Pries-Heje   Roskilde University, Denmark

SCIS 2014 Program Committee

Margunn Aanestad, Norway
Karin Axelsson, Sweden
Jeffry Babb, USA
Pernille Bjørn, Denmark
Claus Bossen, Denmark
Bendik Bygstad, Norway
Jan Damsgaard, Denmark
Sara Eriksen, Sweden
Miria Grisot, Norway
Karin Hedström, Sweden
Ola Henfridsson, Sweden
Jonny Holmström, Sweden
Netta Iivari, Finland
Pertti Järvinen, Finland
Karlheinz Kautz, Australia
Christina Keller, Sweden
Katarina Lindblad-Gidlund, Sweden

Jan Ljungberg, Sweden
Carl Erik Moe, Norway
Eric Monteiro, Norway
Peter Axel Nielsen, Denmark
Tero Päivärinta, Sweden
Samuli Pekkola, Finland
John S. Persson, Denmark
Matti Rossi, Finland
Ada Scupola, Denmark
Kari Smolander, Finland
Reima Suomi, Finland
Per Svejvig, Denmark
Virpi Tuunainen, Finland
Tuure Tuunanen, Finland
Guri B. Verne, Norway

Table of Contents

Service Design and Coevolution of an Emerging SME Wellness Ecosystem

Elina Annanperä and Kari Liukkunen

University of Oulu, Department of Information Processing Science,
P.O.B. 3000, 90014 University of Oulu, Finland
{Elina.Annanpera,Kari.Liukkunen}@oulu.fi

Abstract. This paper presents the formation of a Finnish SME wellness ecosystem during its first stages. The activities include setting a common vision of the ecosystem, its target state and challenges, as well as the joined service design possibilities. The ecosystem consists of SME companies that are looking to integrate their offer at the technology and service levels. The researchers are facilitating and observing the formation of the ecosystem with workshops and interviews to analyze the ecosystem coevolution and service design possibilities. This paper focuses on the early activities of the coevolution and service design within the ecosystem, the solution packaging from the ecosystem point of view, before the service offerings are tested with the customers. These actions are closely linked to other challenges of forming the SME wellness service ecosystem; these challenges are also being studied and are presented in this paper.

Keywords: Service design, business ecosystem, SME ecosystem, wellness.

1 Introduction

Startups and small companies trying to grow their impact on markets often struggle to get their share of the existing markets. The situation for a new company is even more difficult if the markets are new and customers are not familiar with these new services. This can be the situation in new service market areas that rely on technology that is not yet familiar to the customers. The companies need to make their services visible and the competition is tough.

These small companies benefit from forming alliances and collaborating. These collaborations can be called business ecosystems as defined by Moore [9]. According to Nambisan [11], these days, information technology products and services are developed in ecosystems. In the case of small companies forming a business ecosystem where there is no single leading company, but instead the companies are equal, the collaboration can be called a small and medium enterprise (SME) ecosystem [15]. In SME ecosystems, the companies need to manage their collaboration differently than in ecosystems where there is one leading company. Also, it is considered beneficial that SMEs tend to want to listen to their customers more closely and are able to react and make changes in their development and service

T.H. Commisso et al. (Eds.): SCIS 2014, LNBIP 186, pp. 1–13, 2014.

design process more easily than larger companies [14]. From the ecosystem point of view, the collaboration of SMEs can mean the integration of technologies in order to offer more variety in services to the customers; it can also include collaboration in sales and customer management. The benefits are clear, but there are also challenges starting from bringing together different ways of operating in customer segments to pricing models and technical solutions.

The emergence of issues concerning both technological and service integration can be seen as coming from the overall emergence of the service sciences and understanding that service development and technology development go hand-in-hand these days. Akaka and Vargo [1] point out that characterizing services according to their technology intensives or other characteristics have become outdated—what is more important is to recognize the importance of their value to the consumer. The production of the value can be observed through the coevolution of the ecosystem. Also, during the formation of the ecosystem, the ability of the organizations to establish and sustain common goals may be a factor in predicting the success of the ecosystem [11].

In this study, an SME ecosystem aims to build a coherent service offering to the Finnish wellness markets. The Finnish wellness markets are an evolving industry, worth 2.1 billion euros in 2011 [2]. Wellness services are mainly offered as preventive services to promote the well-being of a person. However, in Finland, wellness services are often offered by bigger companies that offer mainly health care services (medical treatment). Recently, a lot of smaller companies have been established in the field. In this case, the main interest for the companies is in the wellness services paid by the employer to its employees, since the future growth potential is seen in that customer segment.

This study follows two operational years of a wellness SME ecosystem initiative formed by six technology oriented companies and some supporting companies as well as five research institutions. These companies all have their wellness service and related technology solution either already in production or in the development phases. The companies seek to integrate their services at the technology and service levels to have a competitive offer to pursue customers. Our aim was to follow the ecosystem coevolution, identify its challenges and possibilities, understand how the ecosystem decides what direction to take, and determine what kind of ecosystem is finally forming. The researchers acted as facilitators to help the ecosystem organizations to analyze their aims and needs from the ecosystem effort. During this time, four bigger workshops were arranged and interviews were conducted to reach the goals of formation of the ecosystem.

In this paper, the theoretical background of the forming of business ecosystems as well as service design in the ecosystem is discussed. The ecosystem coevolution and decision making regarding the form of ecosystem collaboration and the service offering is elaborated through the results of the workshops and the interviews. Suggestions for next steps and required actions are given and service design outcomes and decisions are discussed. Finally, future work for following the SME ecosystem coevolution is suggested.

2   Service Design in a Business Ecosystem

Ecosystems in the business world can be identified as communities that are supported by the interaction between organizations and individuals [9]. The traditional view in the literature has been that business ecosystems are often formed around one key organization. The most well-known examples of such ecosystems are various information and communication technology (ICT) solution and service manufacturers. For instance, when a customer buys a mobile phone, the manufacturing of the phone itself, the software content, the mobile phone operator, as well as the other value-added content providers form a business ecosystem to provide a mobile solution service for the customer.

Business ecosystems aim to benefit the organizations involved. The organizations bring their own capabilities to the ecosystem to complement the service or product offer of the ecosystem. The benefits of a business ecosystem are seen in the possibilities of growth in the markets the ecosystem operates in; it can be easier for the business ecosystem members to utilize opportunities presented in the markets and present solutions to customer needs [9]. Business ecosystems go through different stages in their life cycles; this is called an evolutionary process, similar to the one in nature [10]. The determinants in the evolutionary process are the organizations supporting and interacting with each other in their service design process as well as exchanging knowledge and resources. The evolutionary process may best be seen by observing the technological integration and the architecture built around the service (the changes that are made by one or more actors in the ecosystem to the ecosystem architecture) [12]. In SME ecosystems, challenges arise during the formation of the service offering, or service solution that would cater to the needs of the customers. These challenges include the decisions about the technical integration and the service architecture. Other challenges of forming an SME ecosystem are in defining common policies, possibly even in sales and customer care, and in the openness and confidentiality issues between organizations and toward their customers. These issues have not been part of a large discussion in the business ecosystem literature thus far.

Characteristic of the business ecosystems are the roles that have been found to exist within them. Iansiti and Levien [8] have recognized that there are typically "keystones"—the organizations that have a great and driving impact on the ecosystem; they may also be called leaders. "Niche players," on the other hand, are in the supporting role in the ecosystem; however, they are often the ones that are innovative and most value creating actors [10]. Niche players also have a complementary role to the ecosystem. "Dominators" aim to challenge the keystones. "Hub landlords" offer resources. Both are operating out of their own interests mainly and not reciprocally [12]. The formation of the roles in an SME ecosystem will depend on the early service design phases and are likely to change over time. However, SME ecosystem roles and mutual dynamics have not been reported in the business ecosystem literature much thus far.

Service offerings and creating customer value are seen as a service design problem. The service offering needs to fulfill customer needs. One view in the literature is that companies should look at the service design as designing solutions to solve customer needs [7]. In the SME ecosystem setting, service solutions can be found in the favorable combination of available ecosystem services. The combination of needed services or elements that produce the needed result from the customer point of view can be found within the ecosystem.

The service value is seen coming from the customer's side of the service consumption. It is pointed out in the service design literature that companies alone cannot define the value of the service, which makes the service design process complex [5]. The service design process has been described as essentially being a result of the dialogue between the company and the customer [13]. In addition, in the SME ecosystem, the ecosystem members need to have a common understanding about the value the service can bring to the customer, because the customer may not be able to explicitly explain their needs. The companies need to know their market in-depth. Here, Akaka and Vargo [1] point out that as we move from a technology society to a service society, the need to view service design in a different way is evident. Ecosystem research supports the point of view that service logic can be based on integration and application of the resources in the ecosystem as a basis for value creation.

In the SME ecosystem, there may be several defining and value-creating activities in process at the same time, as the organizations are going through iterative processes varying between the overall ecosystem strategy and their own business strategy. The companies are validating their own technology and services at the same time as the joined integrations and service design is going on. This paper addresses the service design within the ecosystem, the possibilities of solution packaging from the ecosystem point of view, before the integration is tested with the customers. These actions are closely linked to other challenges of an emerging SME wellness ecosystem.

3   Research Setting and Methods

The motivation for the SME ecosystem effort can be found in the operational reality of the technology based service business. The organizations in this study were participating in a nationally funded research and development program. The program aims to bring together service enablers and ICT platform owners to develop new digital services into several expert areas, such as the wellness area. The research program acts as an enabler for companies and research institutions with similar interests to collaborate in developing new, innovative technology and services. The participants in these research programs have joined in voluntarily. During the first year of the program, the organizations were working on traditional projects that were focused around one lead company. After a short time, the organizations began to realize they could benefit from a wider collaboration. It was agreed within the program to continue work as a business ecosystem, where the synergies of knowledge, research, and technologies could be combined.

Each participating company operates in the wellness service field in Finland—some of the companies were recent start-ups while other companies were more established by the time the ecosystem coevolution started. The overall focus area of the companies is wellness services and technologies. There were six main companies involved in the ecosystem cooperation directly. Three of these were considered leader companies and three were supporting companies that added expertise to these "keystone" companies. In addition, there were companies that were part of the larger ecosystem, but not part of the research activities described in this paper (i.e., not part of the research program). The companies involved in this SME ecosystem included a company offering a service (and a technical platform) to companies to help them offer employer-supported well-being and recreational services to their employees; two companies developing different mobile applications for personal wellness; a personal medical and wellness information database-related services developer, an activity sensor manufacturer, and a company that was in the process of developing a scorecard-type organizational wellness measurement solution.

In addition to these companies, researchers from five Finnish universities were involved in the formation of the ecosystem. The roles and needs from the research resource were defined during the ecosystem coevolution, but the capabilities of the researchers were aligned with organizational, technical, and information systems expertise that was needed in the ecosystem. The roles of the research institutions were also clear in the sense that the authors of this paper had the service design and ecosystem collaboration in their research interests.

3.1   Research Method

The research method we used was action research. Here, the research is conducted in close collaboration with the organizations, as is typical for action research. In action research, the researcher can attempt to bring change to the organization through learning from it; in this research, the organizational environment is extended to the ecosystem context [6]. Also, planning the interaction and interventions and following the companies' executions of the planned activities is part of the action research design [3]. Action research is a means of making changes in the way the organizations operate [4], and in the case of an ecosystem, the changes affect all of the members of the ecosystem. The interaction between the researchers and the ecosystem's organizations aims to solve the issues that arise in the service design and the ecosystem coevolution. The researchers' role as part of the business ecosystem is to take part in the ecosystem coevolution, identify problems, and provide potential solutions or problem-solving mechanisms to the ecosystem cooperation. The empirical data for the analysis of the research was collected through four workshops and 11 interviews. The timeline can be seen in Figure 1.

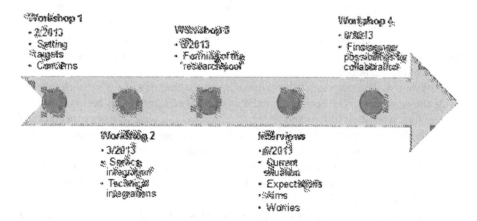

Fig. 1. Research activities and timeline in ecosystem facilitation

The workshops were organized during the year 2013 in four installments. Each arranged workshop was designed to take the business ecosystem coevolution further and strengthen the cooperation between the ecosystem members. Although the ecosystem members became part of the ecosystem for their own interests, organizing the cooperation in the beginning and getting to know each other was planned and facilitated by the authors of this paper. The other researchers involved in the ecosystem participated in these workshops as members of the ecosystem, bringing their own interests and capabilities into the mix with the companies. The themes of the workshops were as follows.

Workshop 1: The first workshop was arranged to meet all of the ecosystem members; there were 18 persons present from 12 organizations. After the introductory round, the participants were asked to form teams to sketch out the target state of the wellness business ecosystem, i.e. something the members would like to see forming out of the collaboration. The ecosystem members were also asked to express their concerns about the future collaboration. The workshop lasted for four hours, the sketching of the ecosystem scenarios was done on paper, and the discussion on the sketches and concerns were recorded.

Workshop 2: This workshop was to start planning for service integrations. Ecosystem members were brought together to discuss and visualize how the components of the ecosystem (the services and available platforms) could be presented from the technical and service points of view. The workshop lasted for two hours and also included the discussion about ongoing integrations and user piloting planning. Altogether, there were altogether nine people from seven organizations. After the workshop, the participants were sent a visualization proposition of the ecosystem services for their commentary that was prepared by the organizing researchers.

Workshop 3: This workshop was themed to map out the use of the research resources involved in the ecosystem. The ecosystem company members were asked to list needs and expectations for the researchers. Similarly, the researchers were asked to list needs and expectations from the companies. The workshop aimed at the formation of a "researcher pool" for the ecosystem in which the researchers would become integrated into the wellness ecosystem with their capabilities. Further, research themes that were important for the companies in the near future were agreed upon. The duration of this workshop was two hours. There were 11 people present from eight organizations.

Workshop 4: The purpose of this workshop was to find new ways to work together inside the ecosystem. The ecosystem members had been interviewed between this and the previous workshop (three) and they had expressed the wish to gather together and try to think of innovative possibilities to further cooperation. This workshop was arranged so that from the initial discussion, a theme was picked for two groups to think of solutions to increase the level of cooperation and visibility of the ecosystem's service offering. This workshop lasted for four hours. Ten people from nine organizations participated in this workshop.

The interviews took place in June 2013. The aim of the interviews was to find out the ecosystem members' situations, expectations, worries, and aims in regard to the ecosystem cooperation. The first author of this paper conducted the interviews. Both companies and university members were interviewed. There were 10 interviews overall, and interviewees six and seven, as shown in Table 1, were interviewed together. The interviewed researchers were asked to think of their role as part of the ecosystem.

Table 1. List of persons interviewed

#	Position within the organization	Organization
1	Chief operational officer	Company A
2	Co-founder, CEO	Company B (start-up)
3	Co-founder, CEO	Company C (start-up)
4	CEO	Company D
5	Founder, CEO	Company E (start-up)
6	Director	Company F
7	Sales director	Company F
8	Researcher	University A
9	Researcher	University B
10	Researcher	University C
11	Researcher	University D

The question themes were based on the business ecosystem coevolution stages as defined by Moore [9]. The emphasis was on the early stages of ecosystem coevolution. The themes from the stages were as follows: the ecosystem service offering, the key markets and customer segments, the kinds of business process architecture we should create, preferred revenue logic, and what participants see as challenges. In addition, we were interested in the different policies and "rules" that the ecosystem members thought were necessary for cooperation and for expanding the ecosystem. The interviews were structured so that the topics moved from company-specific information to ecosystem possibilities.

The interviews were performed via Skype and recorded. The length of the interviews was between 30 to 60 minutes. The interviews were analyzed by the themes that emerged from the questions and conversations. The style was a themed interview, and the interest was focused on the general opinions and solution suggestions the interviewees had of this formation of the ecosystem.

4   Wellness Ecosystem Coevolution and Service Design

At the beginning of the SME wellness ecosystem coevolution, there was only a selection of interested organizations. The organizations needed to be brought together to start building trust between the organizations. Research organizations at this phase are a natural leading organization and facilitator to take the initiative to help the companies to find their mutual language.

The ecosystem cooperation and coevolution started by defining the goals the ecosystem had for the short- and long-term. At first, the actors in the ecosystem needed to get to know each other. The key competence and cooperation possibilities needed to be mapped out so that integrations at the technical and service level could be done. Workshops one and two focused on these tasks, and the researchers' role in matching the research capacity and competence each organization would need was part of this phase.

In the beginning, the ecosystem coevolution went through the phases of forming the initial idea of the cooperation to actually starting the first stage of integration and on to higher-level needs, which were expressed in workshop two. The companies expressed the need and interest for common service offerings or a selection of service offerings and common marketing and sales plans and infrastructure. The ecosystem coevolution shows that the decision made within the ecosystem affects the formation of the service design and service offering outcome. The progress of this ecosystem work can be seen in retrospect in the adjusting of the goals as time went by and as ecosystem members got to know each other and started cooperating. In particular, this can be seen through the interviews, as they took place at a time when the organizations had somewhat idealized goals and perceptions of the future possibilities. The ecosystem was still forming and not very stable, some initially interested companies had dropped out of the ecosystem, and the rest were trying to reach a consensus.

The interviewees were asked about their overall vision of this ecosystem and what they thought the ecosystem's target states were, i.e. where the ecosystem was headed in the long run. One interviewee said that this ecosystem could be a basis for a wellness service and technology production, service, and export cluster. In general, the interviewees were hoping the ecosystem collaboration would result in a common customer base and active collaboration that would lead to new innovative service solutions. Also, participants hoped to achieve improved sales skills and increased sales as a result of this collaboration so that customers' needs would be better met. These actions were summed up by one of the interviewees by remarking that the ecosystem needed a common webpage.

The interviewees were also asked about the guidelines and agreements that should be in place among the ecosystem member organizations. Initially, we talked about an ecosystem rulebook, but in the end, common policies are more complex and are based on the common target and vision of the ecosystem, not just on agreements between companies that can be made via legal arrangements. The issues that need a common consensus in general and in particular in the cooperation and interaction with the customers are mutual agreements about the sales functions: If common customers are acquired, how the costs and revenues are shared, how the customer care and contacting should be shared, and which partner takes care of it. Other important issues that needed common policies were mutual trust and confidentiality and openness in matters that concern others. Participants expressed the need for common policies for the publicity of common activities, taking into consideration both the other ecosystem members as well as the customers. One of the interviewees pointed out that we should all realize that we are partners: We are not in competition with each other. It was agreed that new partners can join the ecosystem within the requirements of the project program policy that has been given to the ecosystem by the funding instrument operator.

The challenges for the near future were mostly the challenges of getting the customers for this common endeavor. The challenge in general was meeting customer needs and convincing the customers, in particular the company customers, that wellness is an important investment in their employees' preventive health and well-being. Other challenges were seen as coming from inside the ecosystem and concerned ecosystem collaboration and cooperation. The companies will of course have other business developments going on at the same time, and that is not seen as a problem. However, the companies can have conflicting interests, and fitting the services and technology integrations together could prove a challenge because of different views on what the service packages or ensembles could be. The wellness service field is new in Finland and the channels for sales are not necessarily ready. The other already existing service providers in the field that are not involved or invested in this ecosystem may not want to be involved in any way in collaborations with these organizations.

We found that certain phases of the emerging ecosystem coevolution can be identified from the SME wellness ecosystem. The phases reflect the needs and possibilities for SME organizations and research organizations collaboration and can be seen as an example of an ecosystem coevolution that is strongly supported and facilitated by a research program funding operator and research institutions. However, the coevolution progress in the emerging ecosystem is best visible in the workshops and their goals. The identified phases are shown in Table 2.

Table 2. SME wellness ecosystem coevolution phases

Phase	Key Questions	Characteristics
Getting to know each other	Who are the member organizations? What are each organization's capabilities?	Getting to know each other, finding common interests, expressing worries or challenges.
Forming common goals	What is the common goal and vision in the short and long term?	Envisioning an idealized goal. Starting the integrations.
Setting rules	What needs to be agreed upon to have this cooperation?	Need for common policies to gain trust and collaboration.
Rationalizing	How can the collaboration be done more easily?	The collaborations need to be easier and faster to get ahead of competition.
Streamlining	Does something need to be changed? How are new members integrated into the collaboration?	The ecosystem work has formed and it is starting to grow and gain attention.

At the service design level, the companies were aiming to find ways to collaborate and combine their services in terms of technical integration and service offering. We needed to determine the best method of service offering packaging.

When asked to illustrate more clearly about the interviewees' view of the most favorable solutions for service integrations and how these should be put together, the answers varied. Interviewees that had specific ideas about what kind of service offerings the ecosystem could have, suggested toolkit thinking, where the customer could choose a toolkit that would fit their needs and the pricing would be done according to the tools (i.e., services) the kit included. Another idea along the same lines was to price the units of each service, which could then be combined as needed by the customer. A frequent opinion was that customer needs are essential, and understanding these needs will lead to suitable pricing and service offering options. There were also views that as there are some clearly more technology-oriented and some more service-oriented organizations in the ecosystem, the service organizations should serve as a customer contact facilitator and therefore take the initiative for designing different service combinations for the customers. To organize the services, some ecosystem members suggested that there should be a separate technology layer and a service layer, as there were basically two kinds of companies involved: the ones where the business is based on a technological solution, and the ones who provide metrics for measuring well-being on the personal or organizational level through scorecard-type tools.

Some of the interviewees said that they saw no need for service offerings that would include all the companies in the ecosystem. Instead, they suggested that there would be service packages offering solutions for different needs in the occupational wellness services area. In these customer needs-based solutions, the composition of the service also depends on the price the customer is willing to pay. In the ecosystem workshops, this idea was discussed openly. The ecosystem members were willing to create ready packages; here, we call them "scenarios of use." They describe typical use scenarios of each service or product and are used to help market these solutions.

The ecosystem members decided in workshop four that each company should create a typical user case based on their service; these could be used as a basis of forming common service packages. However, some logical business cases have formed inside the ecosystem. This is due to some companies' business idea to function as a technical platform that can offer accompanied services that attached or integrated. The overall idea of tailoring the services to customer needs has not been forgotten, but several of these supporting or attached services can be offered to the customer via different platforms.

Despite the work we have done and the open discussions, some companies find that their service offering, or technology, fits better with one company over others, and close collaborations have formed. Toward the end of the first stages of cooperation, the ecosystem members started to discuss extending the ecosystem. New companies are joining in, and streamlining the ecosystem for easy integration is the next challenge.

5   Conclusion

The focus of this paper is on the organizational point of view of an emerging SME wellness ecosystem, the formation of the ecosystem, its challenges, as well as the service design process that aims to offer solutions to service integration. The researchers acted as facilitators and can be seen as more neutral partners than other companies, which are at first seen more as competitors. The researchers gained the needed trust by arranging the first meetings and opening the discussion. This soon led to the building of trust between the companies and into the open atmosphere that followed as the ecosystem coevolution progressed. The formation of the ecosystem started by collecting ideas and worries, but also the foreseen benefits and needed common policies concerning collaboration from the organizations. The researchers' role was to help the organizations, analyze these expressed needs and concerns, and combine the knowledge of service design into the business ecosystem.

The companies were committed to work together to gain the benefits of the collaboration from early on, which is important since the commitment cannot be forced by anyone, but instead is voluntary. The interviewees' views about the success of the early stage integrations seemed to vary depending on the role they had assumed in the ecosystem. Some organizations were more actively performing integrations and cooperating with each other; their service and underlying was more developed than others. Those that were more active seemed to also be more content with the pace of the work thus far.

The ecosystem service offering can be modeled using so-called "business case owners," companies that have collected other companies to collaborate via, for example, their technological platform. These organizations are similar to keystone organizations, which are depicted in the business ecosystem literature. Some other companies are actively involved in the ecosystem and may have connections between business cases, with their own customers on the side. These organizations can be seen as the niche players in the ecosystem. The business case view is not restrictive—the companies are freely looking for opportunities outside the business cases, but it is a way to organize the services that are offered to customers.

An initial objective was to find ways to gather all the services in one bundle, but that proved to be an inefficient way of looking at the service offering. The companies came to realize that modeling each service so that others know what everyone is doing and then building user scenarios that logically fit together is a more efficient and customer-friendly approach. The customer point of view to the ecosystem service offering effort has had quite a small role thus far, but the need to get pilot customers to collaborate with the ecosystem to get validation to the service offering is the next step toward coherent service offering all the way to a choosing a business model for the joined services.

The first phases of the ecosystem coevolution have shown that building the cooperation and the trust that leads to openness and recognizing the full potential of the collaboration is taking longer than originally planned. However, these early phases of the ecosystem coevolution are extremely important when we think of the

SMEs in competing fields. The researchers' role as a neutral, but interested partner may help to increase the pace of the cooperation through finding the tools and methods to facilitate the ecosystem cooperation. The meetings and first technology integrations have aided in the process of building that trust and openness, and toward the end of the year, the plans for joining forces in promotion and sales as well as having joined communication strategy have been agreed to. The companies are also planning to collaborate in taking their services to global markets. The realization of these next steps and validating the joined service offering and the business model are the researchers' next challenges in following the ecosystem's evolution. All the while, the ecosystem is expanding; it is taking on new companies, and the challenges in maintaining the trust and openness and fitting the new companies and their services into the existing ecosystem will need some facilitation.

Acknowledgments. This work was supported by TEKES (The Finnish Funding Agency for Technology and Innovation) as part of the Digital Service program of DIGILE (Finnish Strategic Centre for Science, Technology and Innovation in the field of ICT and digital business).

References

1. Akaka, M.A., Vargo, S.L.: Technology as a Operant Recourse in Service (Eco)systems. Systems and E-Business Management (in press), doi:10.1007/s10257-013-0220-5
2. Aura, O., Ahonen, G., Ilmarinen, J.: Strategisen hyvinvoinnin tila Suomessa. Tutkimusraportti. Excenta, Helsinki (2012)
3. Avison, D., Lau, F., Myers, M., Nielsen, P.A.: Action Research. Communications of the ACM 42(1), 94–97 (1999)
4. Baskerville, R., Wood-Harper, A.T.: Diversity in Information Systems Action Research Methods. European Journal of Information Systems 7(2), 90–107 (1998)
5. Evanschitzky, H., Wangenheim, F., Woisetschläger, D.: Service and Solution Innovation: Overview and Research Agenda. Industrial Marketing Management 40(5), 657–660 (2011)
6. Gummeson, E.: Qualitative Methods in Management Research. Sage, Thousand Oaks (2000)
7. Hakanen, T., Jaakkola, E.: Co-Creating Customer-Focused Solutions Within Business Networks: A Service Perspective. Journal of Service Management 23(4), 593–611 (2012)
8. Iansiti, M., Levien, R.: Strategy as Ecology. Harvard Business Review, pp. 1–10 (March 2004)
9. Moore, J.F.: The Death of Competition. Leadership and Strategy in the Age of Business Ecosystems. Harper Collins, New York (1996)
10. Mäkinen, S.J., Dedehayir, O.: Business Ecosystem Evolution and Strategic Considerations: A Literature Review. In: Katzy, B., Holzmann, T., Sailer, K., Thoben, K.D. (eds.) Proceedings of the 2012 18th International Conference on Engineering, Technology and Innovation (2012)
11. Nambisan, S.: Information Technology and Product/Service Innovation: A Brief Assessment and Some Suggestions for Future Research. JAIS 14, 215–226 (2013); April Special Edition

12. Peltoniemi, M.: Preliminary Theoretical Framework for the Study of Business Ecosystems. ECO 8(1), 10–19 (2006)
13. Tuli, K.R., Kohli, A.K., Bharadwaj, S.G.: Rethinking Customer Solutions: From Product Bundles to Relational Process. Journal of Marketing 71(3), 1–17 (2007)
14. Vuorela, T., Ahola, H., Aro, P.: Opportunities and Challenges of Using Service Design in SME Service Business Development. In: Miettinen, S., Valtonen, A. (eds.) Service Design with Theory, HansaBook, Vantaa (2012)
15. Wang, J., De Wilde, P.: Evolution-Generated Communications in Digital Business Ecosystem. In: 2008 IEEE Conference on Cybernetics and Intelligent Systems, pp. 618–623 (2008)

XP in a Small Software Development Business: Adapting to Local Constraints

Jeffry S. Babb[1], Rashina Hoda[2], and Jacob Nørbjerg[3]

[1] Department of Computer Information Decision Management, West Texas A&M University,
2403 Russell Long Blvd. Canyon, Texas, 79016, USA
[2] Department of Electrical and Computer Engineering, University of Auckland
City Campus, Auckland, New Zealand
[3] Department of Computer Science, University of Aalborg
Selma Lagerlöfs Vej 300, 9220 Aalborg Ø, Denmark
jbabb@wtamu.edu, r.hoda@auckland.ac.nz, jacobnor@cs.aau.dk

Abstract. While small software development shops have trended towards the adoption of Agile methods, local conditions and high iteration pressure typically cause adaptations and appropriations of Agile methods. This paper shares evidence from a study concerning how a small software development company adopts and adapts, XP to suit their business. Based on a Dialogical Action Research project, the study reflects on the conditions leading to Agile process adaptation, and why ad hoc and "a la carte" approaches may be problematic. Limitations and drawbacks to aspects of XP are also discussed. The Agile practices most sustainable for small shop teams, with process maintenance and viability as a goal, are highlighted.

Keywords: Agile methods, method adoption, method adaption, local conditions, process evolution.

1 Introduction

Most software development organizations have less than 10 employees. 80% of US software companies and 89% of the IT consultancy and service companies in the Copenhagen and southern Sweden regions belong in this segment [1, 2]. Research into the practices, conditions, specific needs, constraints and challenges of small software development shops is, however, scarce [1, 3-5].

For the purpose of this paper, a small shop is not necessarily identical to a small team. A small team can exist in a small company (hence the term "small shop") or within a larger company. We use the term "small shop" as a term of convenience and also as a term that the practitioners self-identified with in the case. Usually, a small team can be considered as mostly autonomous where the small-shop team would be the most autonomous. However, a small software shop faces specific constraints and conditions which induce particular requirements and limitations on its methods and processes [6]. Unlike the small team operating in a larger company, a small shop does not have access to a support infrastructure; e.g. a quality management department

T.H. Commisso et al. (Eds.): SCIS 2014, LNBIP 186, pp. 14–29, 2014.
© Springer International Publishing Switzerland 2014

which is responsible for adapting new methods and techniques [3, 7, 8]. The economic constraints of a small company more profoundly enforce short intense release cycles with an often-reduced capacity to share knowledge and reflect upon experiences. Furthermore, a dynamic environment together with small diversified projects leaves little room for institutionalizing processes [6].

The Agile approach seems to fit well with the small shop setting [7], but Agile methods are rarely adopted "off the shelf", but rather adapted to fit local circumstances and constraints [4, 9-12]. Previous research into agile adaptation has, however, examined the context larger organizations (50 or more employees) but there is little research into agile adoption and adaptation in small software shops. Larger organizations have the resources and capabilities required for a planned approach to adaptation, but a small software shop will often choose a pragmatic and/or ad hoc approach to process adaptation due to their small size and resource constraints. Therefore, the resulting process may be shaped more by personal idiosyncrasies rather than analysis of the company's needs and capabilities [4].

In this paper we will describe and analyze how a small software shop adopted and adapted the agile method Extreme Programming (XP) in order to address specific issues and challenges in the company. The paper is the outcome of a Dialogical Action Research (DAR) study in a small software shop in the USA. XP was introduced into the small shop in several iterations after an initial diagnosis of the company's characteristics and needs. We characterize the use (adoption and adaptation) of the method and discuss which elements were used and which were discarded or heavily modified. We discuss how the resulting combination of software development work in the case is related to the constraints and conditions of the small software shop. An analysis of the case shows that agile methods, while helpful for small shops to improve their processes and productivity, are modified to meet the unique conditions of a small software shop.

Previous studies have identified a number of organizational and contextual factors influencing the adoption and adaptation of agile methods [10-12, 23, 24]. We supplement these studies by showing how the les-often-studied small shop context shapes XP adoption. In fact, key XP practices and recommendations, such as "having a customer on site" may be structurally incompatible with the small shop environment – and perhaps even in the context of small teams in larger organizations.

This paper also seeks answers to the expressed need for empirical studies of agile development [13, 14]. The study contributes in this regard as it is based on a longitudinal episode of DAR investigating XP adoption and use in a small-team/small-shop context.

The rest of the paper is structured as follows: first, we characterize small shop software development. Next, the process of both adopting and adapting an agile method, XP, is considered. The research method used to investigate the case, Dialogical Action Research, is outlined in terms of how this method was used to achieve the research outcomes. We next characterize how the small shop in the case, SSC, proceeded to adapt and adopt XP. The paper then proceeds to discuss the implications of agile software process adaption, with consideration for implications for theory and practice. The paper then concludes with future directions for the work.

2   Small Shop Software Development

What is now commonly called "traditional" approaches to information systems development, software engineering, and software project management grew out of the needs of large-scale industrial and military software projects; however, currently a significant portion of software products and services are increasingly produced by small teams [3]. Small teams and small projects face conditions and challenges that require methods and processes that sometimes differ from what is required in larger teams and projects [3]. Among these conditions and challenges are: (1) A lack of wider institutional/organization sanction or reinforcement of their practices and habits; (2) Less time or fewer resources to engage a wider community of professionals for reinforcement of good practices and amelioration for less effective habits; (3) A constant focus on delivery due to financial constraints, leaving less time for reflection and learning; (4) Fewer "degrees of freedom," or avenues, from which new practices can be gleaned.

There has been little research into small team software development practices prior to the rise in the importance of personal computer and microcomputers in the 1980s and of Internet-related applications and technologies in the 1990s and 2000s. With the onset of agile software development methods, however, a considerable amount of research and field reports have concentrated on agility in software development with some reports concluding the utility of agile methods is greatest in a small-team context [7].

Small software shops, here defined as software development companies with less than 10 developers, share several of the characteristics of small teams. Like the small team within a larger company, small shops have little need for elaborate plans, change management procedures or document-based coordination and communication in general [14, 15]. However, a small team working in a large company often has access to resources not found in the small company setting. Large companies, for example, may be more apt to provide infrastructure and resources for method and tool support, quality assurance, testing, configuration management, and documentation. A larger organization may also provide training opportunities and access to a pool of knowledge and expertise, as well as institutionalized processes that novice developers can adopt.

Often, the small software shop cannot approach or sustain the support infrastructures and resources of a larger organization [8]. Typically, there are only a few developers with constrained (or non-existent) access to the breadth and depth of experience and knowledge that can be found in a larger organization. Furthermore, practitioners in the small shop may lack a formal background/training in the computing disciplines conducive to software development. Often, the small software shop operates in a highly competitive environment and has few financial resources to spare for training, education, and development beyond what developers undertake in their own time (and using their own resources). Small shop survival hinges on short delivery cycles that produce immediate value to the customer.

Under these circumstances, comprehensive planning, detailed requirements analysis, documentation, and elaborate quality assurance activities mandated by most software development methods cede to release-and-patch strategies, incremental deliveries, and rapid (yet inconsistent) customer feedback [1, 4, 6].

The sum of the constraints faced by small software shops implies that the methods, tools, and techniques traditionally recommended in software engineering, which have been evolved over the long term in the context of the large team and/or large company, do not fit well with the small software company [3, 14, 15, 16]. This does not imply, however, that a small software shop should not strive towards a systematic and professional software development process [6, 14, 15, 16], but that methods and processes used must be adapted to the small-shop environment and constraints; i.e. designed around frequent and incremental deliveries, and a workable channel for rapid customer feedback for revised requirements [3]. The family of agile software development methods, which research has shown to be suited to the small team environment, seems to fit these conditions of the small shop software shop [14, 15].

The paper now turns to the means by which small shops can appropriate innovations, such as Agile methods, given their operating constraints. The small software shop has little time to spend on adopting and adapting a method; i.e. finding the right method, training developers, and creating feedback loops for reflection and adjustments to method use [4]. Thus, we ask how and why these small software shops adopt and adapt innovations such as Agile methods in a manner that is plausible, beneficial, and sustainable to their situation?

3   Adopting and Adapting Agile Methods

Software developers rarely adopt systems and software development methods outright, but rather filter and combine elements from these methods to fit their needs. The criteria for selecting method elements, and the adaptation process itself appears to be complex and dependent on a number of factors, including: 1) the background and experience of the developers; 2) how and with what training a method is introduced to the developers; 3) the organizational context and managerial culture; 4) the application domain, and so forth [17-22]. However, the small shop is usually consumed with existential issues related to product delivery and a steady pipeline of customers will often dictate the terms of adoption and adaptation.

Developers also commonly adapt Agile methods to suit local contexts and conditions [10-12, 23, 24]. Popular agile methods like Scrum and XP recommend regular collaboration with the customer [25, 26]. Research shows, however, that it is very difficult to fulfill this requirement in practice, and many development teams revert to traditional document based communication with the customer or use a "customer proxy" from their own organization who may or may not have access to first-hand knowledge about the customer's needs [10, 23].

Mangalaraj, Mahapatra, and Nerur [12], develop a model to explain organizational acceptance of agile practices. According to the model, individual, team, technological, task, and environmental factors are key influences on organizational acceptance of XP practices. Using the model to analyze two instances of agile practices in the same organization, the authors show how conditions and constraints can vary across teams in the same organization, leading to different ways to implement agile practices.

Cao et al. [24] use Adaptive Structuration Theory (AST) to analyze "[h]ow agile software development methodologies [are] adapted for use in different contexts?" (p. 333). Similar to [23] they find that the development teams will implement a number of adaptation strategies in order to overcome challenges to agile method adoption. The purpose of the adaptation is to maintain the rationale or "spirit" behind the agile methods; e.g., working software, open communication, iterative progress, honest plans, and team agency; within the constraints set by the developers' capabilities and expertise, as well as the conditions of the development project, such as; e.g. complex architectural requirements, the lack of access to a customer, or organizational and management constraints.

Senapathi and Srinivasan [11] explore how innovation, sociological, technological, and organizational factors influence the breadth and depth of agile usage in an organization and the effectiveness of agile methods for the organization.

Any agile practices may be changed or omitted to fit local constraints and conditions [25, 26, 32, 33]. Such adaptations do not, in and by themselves make the resulting practices non-agile, rather the adaptations are motivated by the development teams' ambition to maintain the "spirit" of agile development within the conditions and constraints they are facing [23, 24]. If, for example, documentation level and details are controlled by regulatory demands as in e.g. finance applications, then developers can fit the agile methods to the documentation requirements by producing "just enough" documentation up-front, and finalizing documentation post-hoc, when the product is reasonably stable, instead of abandoning agile practices altogether [24].

4   Research Method

In order to understand the phenomenon of adoption and adaptation of agile methods in a small-shop setting, the research was conducted with Dialogical Action Research (DAR) [27-29]. DAR presents a researcher/practitioner partnership that allows for a reflective dialog to explore and shape change in an organization and also specify learning for a scientific community. For this research, a small software shop, SSC, entered into a DAR partnership with an aim to adopt a suitable software development method and the researcher's aim was to understand the adoption/adaption process from an empirical perspective. Taking the DAR approach requires that the researcher engage in dialog with the practitioner to identify unexpected issues and react accordingly with suggestions for action-taking to effect change. This emergent and engaged approach for both research and practice is designed to foster greater understanding of practical phenomenon, such as the adoption and adaption of agile methods [30]. DAR, as is the case with agile methods, is intended to be engaged iteratively such that a practitioner's real-world problem can be addressed through dialog, action planning, action taking and assessment [27].

The engagement with SSC took place over a period of nine months from June 2008 to February 2009. In the first phase of the research the following steps were carried out (1) plausibility; (2) diagnosis; (3) prescription. This resulted in a diagnosis of the main problems experienced by the practitioners in SSC. Understanding SSC's desire for a valid software development method, the researcher suggested and confirmed the suitability of agile methods and XP in particular within the DAR partnership. Also during the DAR partnership, the researcher monitored the progress of two major projects, and myriad smaller projects, to better understand SSC's adopted and adapted XP practices.

The practitioner-researcher partnership at SSC was used as a source of data that primarily consisted of research field notes, interview and meeting transcripts and supplemental documents taken from the practitioners' work environment. Using HyperResearch these texts were coded, using open, axial, and selective coding, in order to derive common themes related to SSC's method adoption, adaptation and use.

5   SSC's Adoption of XP

The DAR partnership at SSC revealed a development process largely consistent with the "waterfall" Systems Development Lifecycle (SDLC).   However, the lead developer and owner, Daphne, felt the need to adopt a method that projected greater professionalism to customers. Dialog also revealed Daphne's perspective that she was the primary arbiter of institutional and problem-domain knowledge and that this knowledge was not effectively shared with the rest of the organization. Daphne characterized this as an immense pressure to be involved in almost all activities in the company, including training new employees and overseeing their work. This became less and less feasible as the company started to grow.

Further dialog and diagnosis culminated in the adoption of XP as a systematic framework for development. The researcher saw value in XP for its reflection and learning components. XP was selected to address the need for a shared and systematic approach to development, and to improve knowledge transfer, learning and reflection within the small shop. Thus, XP was selected for two primary reasons: (1) it was the most appealing to SSC's practitioners after a presentation of alternative Agile mehods, and (2) it presented Daphne with an opportunity to work closely with the three other developers and one graphic artist.

Over time, the practices and techniques of XP were introduced gradually into SSC by the researcher. The first to be introduced were Daily Standup Meeting and User Stories. According to Daphne, these activities provided the team with increased focus and increased productivity. Spike Solutions were also useful to SSC as they afforded justification for experimentation and testing. Next, SSC tried pair programming mainly as a means to create Spike Solutions whenever uncertainty was encountered.

Figure 1 shows the major processes that SSC made an attempt to adopt. In Figure 1-3, the elements outlined in solid black are those that SSC were able to fully and successfully adopt. The elements outlined as dashed are those that were partially adopted or adapted. Lastly, any element outlined as dotted are those where were not adopted at all.

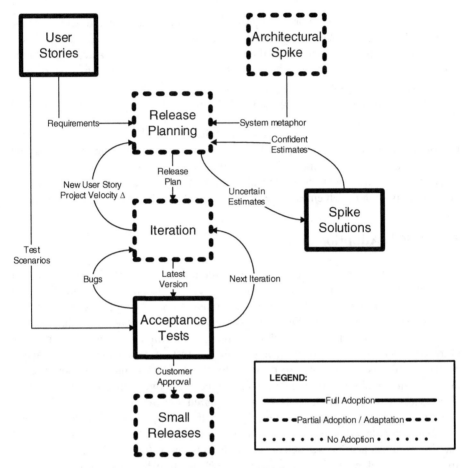

Fig. 1. SSC's Adoption of XP Processes

Initially, SSC focused on adopting the XP processes related to Iteration Planning. Figure 2 shows the Iteration activities SSC were able to fully or partially adapt. As a next step, SSC had progressed further with learning and adopting XP and responded with positive feedback concerning the benefits of adopting XP. Toward the end of the study, SSC had adopted the Collective Code Ownership portions of the XP method. At this stage differences in the nature of SSC's web development projects and other impediments arose which prevented SSC from fully adopting the XP activities within Collective Code Ownership. When the researcher suggested that XP encourages all production code to be written using Pair Programming, SSC responded that it would not be possible to do so given the vast number of projects simultaneously underway.

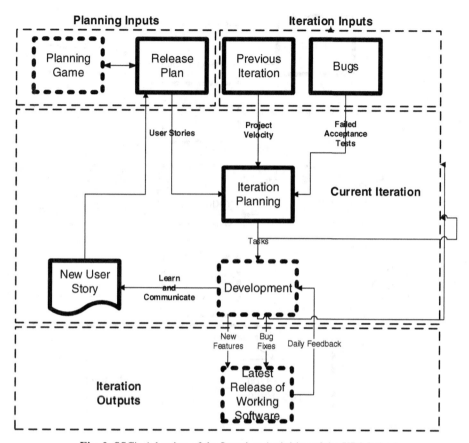

Fig. 2. SSC's Adoption of the Iteration Activities of the XP Method

Similarly, toward the end of the study, the researcher saw no direct evidence that Unit Testing was implemented in the manner suggested by XP. This was despite the fact that the researcher demonstrated to the SSC developers how to do Unit Testing with the NUnit software package. As shown in Figure 3 (dotted line means no adoption), the principle of Move People Around was not adequately considered or attempted save for the times when two developers would "pair" to create a Spike Solution. Lastly, none of the principle of Release Planning activities, such as Acceptance Testing and automated Unit Testing procedures, were witnessed or documented by the researcher.

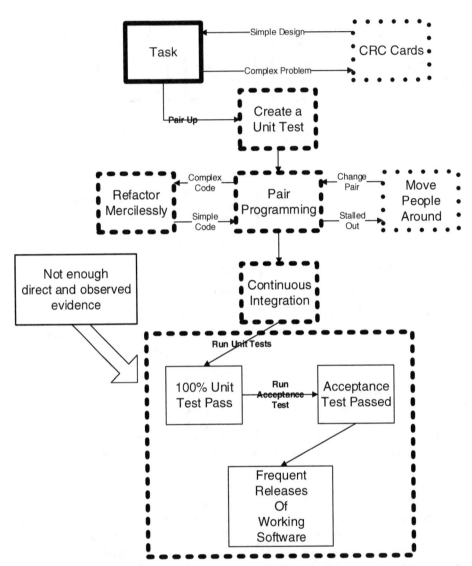

Fig. 3. SSC's Adoption of the Collective Code Ownership Activities of the XP Method

By the end of the study period, SSC had learned and/or tried the majority of XP practices and offered the researcher substantial positive feedback about their successes with using the method and also reported areas where the method was not going to "fit" them. Figure 4 summarizes SSCs adoption and adaptation of XP.

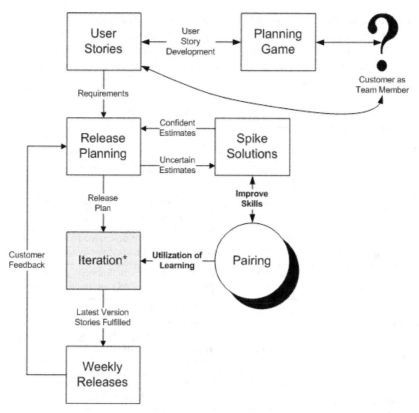

Fig. 4. XP Processes as Adapted by SSC

6   Analysis and Discussion

SSC's adoption and adaption are consistent with suggestions that a team that appropriates XP should "disaggregate" the elements of XP and subsequently critically examine the value of each element [25, 33, 34]. Moreover, local adaptation is also predicted and encouraged as part and parcel of a team taking responsibility for its own process management and evolution [25]. Coleman [22] suggests that small companies will tend to rely on tacit knowledge and less formal means of communication and documentation. In most cases, the burden of the formalizations of method will be difficult to adopt in the small shop setting.   It is important to reiterate that both informal learning structures, a natural tendency for Daphne to keep the "reins of control" in tight, and high iteration pressure were primary influences on the adoption and adaptation experiences of SSC.

In Table 1 below, we summarize the outcomes of SSC's adoption and adaption of XP. SSC was particularly interested in the XP practices that were perceived to be immediately useful and/or consistent with their overall desire to adopt a method: the ability to explain their process to customers, and as a vehicle for knowledge sharing and learning. Prior to XP adoption/adaptation, SSC felt as though they were wasting time by not learning from past projects and that they had generally fallen into a routine that followed a plan-code-test-release cycle without any formalization. Given this low bar, it is possible that any structured approach offered would have been welcomed, agile or not. However, in the case of SSC, the structure and discipline of XP was innovation enough.

Table 1. Summary of SSC's adoption and adaption of XP

XP Practice	Outcome	Implications
User Stories	Adopted	Valued as a means for feature documentation.
Planning Game	Adopted	Used to iteratively refine user stories. Maintained physically on cards.
Architectural Spike	Adapted	System metaphor discussed inconsistently. It is not likely this practice survived.
Release Planning	Adapted	High number of simultaneous projects prevented consistent care in release planning.
0Spike Solutions	Adopted	Perhaps more adopted. Proof of concept spike projects were used for junior developers to prove feasibility to lead developer.
Weekly Release	Adapted	High number of simultaneous projects prevented consistent weekly releases.
Daily Standup	Adopted	Eventually valued for task assignment and coordination. Also used for reflection activities.
Unit Testing	Adapted	Not consistently used but was incorporated in a few projects. It is not likely this practice survived.
Refactor Mercilessly	Adapted	Discussed intermittently during standup. Dedicated tracking and use of tools not observed. It is not likely this practice survived.
Pair Programming	Adapted	Used as a means of training junior developers in "how things are done." Use for bidirectional learning and reflection not observed.
CRC (Class, Responsibilities, Collaboration) Cards	Omitted	While user story cards were seen as useful, the team thought these to be cumbersome.
Move People Around	Omitted	High number of simultaneous projects and team size made this prohibitive.
Continuous Integration	Adapted	Inconsistently implemented. Many projects would go for weeks without integrating "done" software into the overall project.
Customer as Team Member	Omitted	High number of simultaneous projects and nature of the business made this very difficult/impossible.

Whereas XP values working software, open communication, iterative progress, honest plans, and team agency, a small shop like SSC ultimately valued the quicker cycles and frequent review of projects to establish their progress. Team learning and agency were often less of a focus. During dialogs, which provided a time for reflection for the team and the individuals, aspects related to learning and empowerment felt compelling to the team. However, during normal working routines, iteration pressure was paramount and the reflective aspects of XP were less engaged.

Adaption raises questions regarding the consequences for deviations from "canonical" XP. Particular interest arises as to why SSC adopted, adapted, or omitted XP practices, and what implications this has for SSC's effectiveness, technical growth, learning, and process maintenance/evolution. Our analysis will focus on two important factors influencing SSC's adoption and adaption of XP: Management attitude and commitment and the characteristics of small software shops.

6.1 Management Attitudes and Commitment

XP adoption at SSC was heavily influenced by the experience and attitude of Daphne, the company owner. She saw the Daily Standup Meetings as a convenient way to monitor project progress, but they were also an important vehicle for sharing knowledge and experience. Similarly, and citing her own higher skill and experience level, she saw Spike Solutions and Pair Programming as means to elevate her employees' skills until parity with her own skills was reached. Further, since she fully expected the skills of her employees to eventually surpass her own, she saw Pair Programming as a means of transferring skills when new problems required her expertise. Thus, an important goal of the DAR partnership was met for Daphne: relief from the pressure of her previous monopoly on knowledge and expertise.

However, while Daphne understandably values control, methods such as XP may pose the risk of Daphne losing direct control over creativity and innovation at SSC. Thus, while Daphne did not support Pair programming as a general practice for knowledge development and Shared Code Ownership, she did support it as a means for transferring her skills to the developers. The impact of management attitudes and commitment is also reported in other research into agile adoption; c.f. [11]. It is possible that this perspective would have evolved over time.

6.2 Being a Small Software Shop

SSC context, as a small software shop, was the primary reason for modifications and adaptation of several elements of XP. Among the more challenging aspects of XP to adopt was the concept of Customer as Team Member. SSC had, at any given time, anywhere from 20 to 40 projects underway; each at varying stages of completion or maintenance. However, SSC did see the utility in this approach in the case of larger projects and in use with their strategic partnerships.

The impracticality of including a customer as team member on every project had follow-on effects and implications for User Stories, Acceptance Testing and the Planning Game. Daphne would write User Stories, and later Acceptance Tests, based on her own notes or her memory of a client's intentions rather than capturing these intentions directly in the user's words (and in their own hand-writing if possible). In short, it was readily apparent that SSC would not be able to follow the orthodoxy of XP in this regard.

The large number of simultaneous projects had effects on Iteration Planning and Release Planning as well. SSC was forced to provide frequent releases of working software on a schedule that is more rigid than XP intends. Furthermore, SSC, did not adopt "test first" or "test driven" Unit Testing. This was despite the fact that the developers did recognize and profess value in the approach – one aptly called it "testing memory." However, it is very probable that SSC will move on towards a "test first" approach over time as they mature with the process.

The SSC developers made significant strides with Pair Programming during the latter period of the study. However, given the very small size of the SSC development team, it was nearly impossible to use Pair Programming to create all production code, as is prescribed by "orthodox" XP practices [25, 32, 33].

XP practices such as Customer as Team Member and Pair Programming are almost always tweaked or adapted one way or the other [36] for a variety of reasons. In the case of SSC, however, we see the adaption of these practices as directly related to the small size of the company.

Other reports of agile development teams relate the adaption (or omission) of the practice of Customer as Team Member to issues in the customer or user organization: the customer organization does not want to commit a person due to resource constraints or a lack of understanding of what it takes to get involved in agile projects or, it is not possible to identify the right representative in the case of; e.g., product development [10, 23]. In the small shop setting, however, the adaption of Customer as Team Member is caused by the large number of individual customers. It would simply not be feasible, given that each developer worked in small increments on different projects for several customers, to have the customer on site.

Regarding Pair Programming, the characteristics of SSC as a small company similarly creates barriers to adopting this practice. Others have related adaption or omission of Pair Programming to lack of interest [24] or to an uneven distribution of knowledge and skills among developers and the need for specialized skills in different parts of the software [12]. In, SSC, however, the practice of pair programming (and other aspects of collective code ownership) was ultimately abandoned because of the nature of the company's projects and customers. Most projects were relatively small and carried out by one developer only. This eroded the need for shared knowledge about a specific project or customer; or, at least, made it very uneconomical to insist on Pair Programming. Note, however, that Daphne would use Pair Programming to ensure other developers were in-sync with her wishes/techniques.

To summarize, the DAR experience affords insight on how certain aspects of XP appear less compatible with the small shop than with teams in a larger organization. While many agile methods may seem "informal" compared to plan-driven methods (such as CMMI), agile methods may present a higher degree of formality than a very small team, such as SSC's developers, can bear. Practices such as Customer on Site and Pair Programming are quite difficult when there are only 3 to 5 developers. While agile may not be "plan-driven" it is certainly an endeavor that requires discipline. Thus, a small shop may naturally "teeter" on the precipice of agility and devolution into ad hoc cowboy coding [35]. It is clear from their adoption and adaption choices that SSC desires the cohesion of team activities, but the characteristics of SSC make consistent teamwork within the XP method a challenge.

Even with XP as a guide, the process formation (adoption and adaption) at SSC was certain to be shaped and tailored by local circumstances and constraints. Coleman [22] proposes that this method tailoring is a normal aspect of process evolution. SSC's challenge will be to establish a means for reflective monitoring of this evolution.

7 Analysis and Discussion

In this paper we have presented a detailed account of how a small software business adopted and adapted XP practices in their development. Of interest in this paper are the motivations for adopting and adapting XP. In the case discussed in this paper, method adaptation happened nearly immediately and in result of the DAR partnership. Some aspects of XP (pair programming in particular) were roundly rejected and only begrudgingly incorporated, sporadically, as a means of engaging in reflection and/or training from manager to developer.

SSC's adoption and adaptation of XP shares many characteristics found in other studies of agile practice. We do, however, also observe how specific circumstances and constraints related to the small size of the company affect XP adoption and use. As such, this paper extends previous research on the adoption and adaptation of agile methods into the domain of small software shops. Understanding the motivations for adaption, and whether adaption choices may miss some of the helpful aspects of an agile method, is also a primary interest and contribution of this paper.

The outcomes and analyses of the DAR partnership has implications for both research and practice: We now have more empirical context for which practices are suitable in a small software shop, but further longitudinal inquiry into adoption and adaption in small shops and small teams is required. There are more questions in need of answering. For instance, during adoption and adaption, are developers aware of the "agile values" and principles or are they "just" performing the steps? How much indoctrination of agile principles and values is needed in order to create sustained support for agile development? What is the role of self-organization in method adoption and adaptation in the small shop? This research also questions the meaning of "team" in small shop agile development. The developers in SSC worked on different projects and thus hardly formed a "team" in the traditional sense. Nevertheless they successfully used team-based agile practices, such as daily stand-up, as a coordination and knowledge sharing mechanism. Further empirical study is required to develop answers, and theorizing, according to these questions.

References

1. Babb, J.S.: Towards A Reflective-Agile Learning Model and Method in the Case of Small-Shop Software Development: Evidence From An Action Research Study. Information Systems, PhD, pp. 449. Virginia Commonwealth University, Richmond VA (2009)
2. Hansen, P.A., Serin, G.: The Structure of the ICT Sector in the Øresund region. ÖresundIT (2010)
3. Fayad, M.E., Laitinen, M., Ward, R.P.: Thinking Objectively: Software Engineering in Small Companies. Commun. ACM 43, 115–118 (2000)
4. Pedreira, O., Piattini, M., Luaces, M.R., Brisaboa, N.R.: A Systematic Review of Software Process Tailoring. ACM SIGSOFT Software Engineering Notes 32, 1–6 (2007)
5. Pino, F.J., Garcia, F., Piattini, M.: Software process improvement in small and medium software enterprises: a systematic review. Software Quality Control 16, 237–261 (2008)
6. Babb, J.J., Nørbjerg, J.: A Model for Reflective Learning in Small Shop Agile Development. In: Molka-Danielsen, J., Nicolajsen, H.W., Persson, J.S. (eds.) Engaged Scandinavian Research. Selected Papers of the Information Systems Research Seminar in Scandinavia, vol. 1, pp. 23–38. Tapir Akademisk Forlag, Molde (2010)
7. Dybå, T.: Factors of Software Process Improvement Success in Small and Large Organizations: An Empirical Study in the Scandinavian Context. In: ESEC/FSE, pp. 148–157. ACM, Helsinki (2003)
8. Laitinen, M., Fayad, M.E., Ward, R.P.: Guest Editors' Introduction: Software Engineering in Small Companies. IEEE Software 17, 75–77 (2000)
9. Nerur, S., Mahapatra, R., Mangalaraj, G.: Challenges of migrating to agile methodologies. Commun. ACM 48, 72–78 (2005)
10. Hoda, R., Noble, J., Marshall, J.: The impact of inadequate customer collaboration on self-organizing Agile teams. Information and Software Technology 53, 521–534 (2011)
11. Senapathi, M., Srinivasan, A.: Understanding post-adoptive agile usage: An exploratory cross-case analysis. The Journal of Systems and Software 85, 1255–1268 (2012)
12. Mangalaraj, G., Mahapatra, R., Nerur, S.: Acceptance of software process innovations – the case of extreme programming. European Journal of Information Systems 18, 344–354 (2009)
13. Dybå, T., Dingsøyr, T.: Empirical studies of agile software development: A systematic review. Information and Software Technology 50, 833–859 (2008)
14. Abrahamsson, P., Conboy, K., Wang, X.: 'Lots done, more to do': the current state of agile systems development research. European Journal of Information Systems 18, 281–284 (2009)
15. Lester, N.G., Wilkie, F.G., McFall, D., Ware, M.P.: Investigating the role of CMMI with expanding company size for small- to medium-sized enterprises. J. Softw. Maint. E 22, 17–31 (2010)
16. Staples, M., Niazi, M., Jeffery, R., Abrahams, A., Byatt, P., Murphy, R.: An exploratory study of why organizations do not adopt CMMI. J. Syst. Softw. 80, 883–895 (2007)
17. Bansler, J.P., Bødker, K.: A Reappraisal of Structured Analysis: Design in an Organizational Context. ACM Transactions on Information Systems 11(2), 165–193 (1993)
18. Stolterman, E.: How System Designers Think about Design and Methods. Some Reflections Based on an Interview Study. Scandinavian Journal of Information Systems 3, 137 (1991)
19. Fitzgerald, B., Russo, N.L., Stolterman, E.: Information Systems Development. Methods in Action. McGraw-Hill (2002)

20. Madsen, S., Kautz, K., Vidgen, R.: A framework for understanding how a unique and local IS development method emerges in practice. European Journal of Information Systems 15, 225–238 (2006)
21. Kautz, K., Madsen, S., Nørbjerg, J.: Persistent Problems and Practices in Information Systems Development. ISJ (2007) (accepted for publication)
22. Coleman, G., O'Connor, R.: Investigating software process in practice: A grounded theory perspective. J. Syst. Softw. 81, 772–784 (2008)
23. Hoda, R., Kruchten, P., Noble, J., Marshall, J.: Agility in Context. Object-Oriented Programming, Systmes, Languages and Applications conference (OOPSLA2010). ACM, Reno/Tahoe (2010)
24. Cao, L., Mohan, K., Xu, P., Ramesh, B.: A framework for adapting agile development methodologies. European Journal of Information Systems 18, 332–343 (2009)
25. Beck, K., Andres, C.: Extreme programming explained: embrace change. Addison-Wesley Professional (2004)
26. Schwaber, K., Beedle, M.: Agile software development with Scrum. Prentice Hall Upper Saddle River (2002)
27. Mårtensson, P., Lee, A.S.: Dialogical Action Research at Omega Corporation. MIS Quarterly 28 (2004)
28. Sein, M.K., Henfridsson, O., Purao, S., Rossi, M., Lindgren, R.: Action Design Research. MIS Quarterly 35 (2011)
29. Costello, G.J., Donnellan, B., Conboy, K.: Dialogical Action Research as Engaged Scholarship: An Empirical Study. In: ICIS (Year)
30. Van de Ven, A.H.: Engaged Scholarship: A Guide for Organizational and Social Research: A Guide for Organizational and Social Research. Oxford University Press (2007)
31. Lee, A.S., Mårtensson, P.: Dialogical Action Research at Omega Corporation, Richmond, VA, pp. 1–39 (2004)
32. Jeffries, R., Anderson, A., Hendrickson, C.: Extreme programming installed. Addison-Wesley Professional (2001)
33. McBreen, P.: Software craftsmanship: the new imperative. Addison-Wesley Professional (2002)
34. Glass, R.L.: The state of the practice of software engineering. IEEE Software 20, 20–21 (2003)
35. Wood, W.A., Kleb, W.L.: Exploring XP for scientific research. IEEE Software 20, 30–36 (2003)
36. Arisholm, E., Gallis, H., Dyba, T., Sjoberg, D.I.: Evaluating pair programming with respect to system complexity and programmer expertise. IEEE Transactions on Software Engineering 33, 65–86 (2007)

Wrestling with Social Media
on Information Systems' Home Ground

Lars Haahr

Information Systems Research Group, Department of Business Administration,
School of Business and Social Sciences, Aarhus University, Denmark
larsh@asb.dk

Abstract. While there are many possible approaches and areas of research for the study of social media, a review shows that only a few of these are used in extant information systems literature. The paper therefore suggests that increased awareness of the possibilities can strengthen research in social media. It is also suggested that information systems scholars can strengthen their interdisciplinary position by making the information systems discipline itself the home ground for research about social media. To address the issue of possible approaches and areas of research, the paper develops a framework that includes conceptual framing and methodology as well as research areas in the information systems discipline. First, the framework guides a review of extant literature about external social media. Going forward, the framework facilitates the development of a future research agenda about social media on information systems home ground.

Keywords: Social media, review, information systems discipline, dialectics.

1 Introduction

The recent years' uprise in research about social media has made it relevant to examine what research approaches have been used in the past and thereby prepare those to be used in the future. Such an awareness of the importance of research approaches has characterized the information systems (IS) discipline since its origin [1, 2] because the employed approach highly impact what questions will be asked, how they are investigated and thereby what research contributions will be provided [3].

In addition to the issue of methodology and theory, the area of research itself is also of importance [3, 4]. Following Avgerou's [5] classification of IS areas of research, the IS discipline includes as diverse areas as organizational application of information technology, the process of systems development, and the societal impact of IS. Therefore the awareness of the area of research is also of utmost importance for the contributions of the IS discipline to the study of social media.

To address these issues, I conducted a systematic review of extant IS literature about social media in eight major IS journals and in the proceedings from the International Conference on Information Systems (ICIS) 2013. To guide the review, a

T.H. Commisso et al. (Eds.): SCIS 2014, LNBIP 186, pp. 30–43, 2014.

framework that focuses on both conceptual framework and methodology as well as on the area of research has been developed.

The review shows that while there are many possible approaches for the study of social media, only a few of the possible conceptual frameworks and methodologies are used in extant IS literature. The review furthermore shows that while there are many possible areas of research as well as actors in the field of social media to focus on, only a few of these areas and actors are focal object in extant IS literature about social media.

Looking forward, the paper therefore suggests an agenda that complements and forwards extant literature by prioritizing multi-stage process studies based in case studies that focuses on organizations' use of social media. Furthermore the paper suggests to prioritize an investigation of the methodological implications of emerging forms of digital trace data.

Seen from an interdisciplinary perspective, a quick perusal of literature about social media in related research disciplines shows that scholars of innovation management in particular have focused on user communities [6, 7] - that scholars of marketing have studied how users' interaction in a virtual setting can be managed [8, 9] - that corporate communication scholars have studied how policies govern and drive the success of employees' participation [10, 11] - and that organization scholars have studied how emerging social technologies take part in changing the fabric of today's organizations [12].

In this interdisciplinary field, it can be advantageous for IS scholars establish a differentiated strategy and research position. To accomplish this objective and to make it a continued learning process, the paper suggests to study social media by drawing on extant IS literature and research areas and thereby get the advantages of home ground.

A necessary delimitation of the present paper comes from the fact that the term social media has become an umbrella term for a diversity of emerging social technologies. Despite the relevance of all contextual implementations of social technologies, this paper solely focuses on external social media in order to ensure a detailed analysis and differentiation of research contributions. .

The purpose of the paper is to characterize extant IS literature about social media with regard to area of research, conceptual framework and methodology, and in continuation of this review to suggest a future agenda for IS research in social media.

The paper proceeds in three major steps. First, I introduce extant IS literature related to social media and then develop a framework for the review and future agenda. Second, I present the employed methodology and the findings of the review. Third, I discuss the findings of the review and suggest possible elements to future IS research about social media.

2   Social Media and Review Framework

This section first introduces social media and second presents the analytical framework for the review.

2.1   Social Media

The last decade has created an uprise in social media platforms like Facebook, Twitter, LinkedIn, etc. The specific platforms are new and continue to renew themselves in an ongoing innovation process. However, the platforms are also already a known phenomenon when regarded as a result of changes in the large digital infrastructure and changes in social interactions sustained by information systems. These changes have been going on for at least two decades and have been studied as such by IS scholars, however not under the heading of social media or with specific focus on social media platforms.

Recent calls for special issues about social media have pointed to information systems as systems of symbols and exchange and pointed to the fact that IS research from the very origin has understood information systems as systems for social interaction [13]. Seen as a historical development of information systems, the relational and social dimension has been pointed to as business opportunity [14–16].

Social media as management fashion: Already when social media emerged as phenomena under the headline of Web 2.0, IS scholars asked whether this was a passing hype or a management fashion that would survive and become anchored in daily practices [17]. A recent study of the discourse of social media in whitepapers from technology vendors points to an instrumental understanding of social media as information systems [18] and thereby continues a robust IS tradition for understanding emerging phenomena as potentially a management fashion [19, 20].

One of the icons of social media, Facebook, has been used to illustrate how digital infrastructures today go beyond organizational boundaries and must be analyzed as an IT artifact in its own right [21] in order to conceptualize for example its generative capability [22] and embedded paradoxes of change and control [21]. Concerning organizations' stakes in social media, also here a robust stream of research exists in how firms exploit communities [23], how the interactive Internet challenges internal knowledge networks [24], and how organizations are forced to navigate in-between a community-centric and an organization-centric approach [15, 25, 26].

The above mentioned examples indicate that although not directly predicated as research in social media, it is possible to draw on a groundswell of extant IS literature in order to study the very latest innovations in the field of social media.

2.2   Review Framework

In order to conduct a structured review of extant IS literature about social media and to establish a future agenda for IS research about social media, the paper employs an analytical framework that takes the fundamental questions about research approaches into account.

Drawing on a robust tradition in IS research for focusing on research approaches [1, 2], it is the aim of the paper to review extant IS literature about social media concerning research area, conceptual framework as well as methodology. In continuation of Chiasson et al. [3, 4], I draw on Avgerou's [5] introduction to IS research. The review thereby includes the concept centric approach recommended by

Webster and Watson [27] and focus on the methodological foundations as in seminal studies of IS research [2, 28, 29] . In order to highlight the IS specific dimension, the framework furthermore includes a focus on the area of research. The inclusion of all three dimensions on the one hand leaves less place for a detailed investigation of the conceptualizations at stake in IS research about social media [27]. On the other hand, it is relevant to examine extant IS literature about social media in all three dimensions due to its very recent uprise. In the following paragraphs I introduce the three dimensions in detail.

Concerning the dimension of research area, I started the review by drawing on Avgerou's classification of research areas within the IS discipline: Applications of IT to support the functioning of an organization, the process of systems development, IS management, the organizational value of IS, and the societal impact of IS. However, due to the results of the review that showed a dominance of user focused studies and informed by Aral et al. [30] that there is a paucity of focus on firms and technology vendors in current research, I found it relevant to change the analytical lens and systematically investigate which actors in the field are the focal object in extant IS literature about social media. By drawing on institutional theory about actors in the organizational field [31, 32] and on a framework for social media [33], I constructed the following exploratory list of actors in the field of social media: User community, professional organizations, technology vendors, consultancies, and media.

The examination of conceptual framework employed the epistemological distinction between variance studies and process studies. Central characteristics are that variance studies emphasize immaterial time ordering and explanations based on necessary and sufficient causality. Process studies emphasize material time ordering and explanations based on necessary but not sufficient causes [1], [34].

Concerning the examination of methodological foundations, I use the methodologies presented in the seminal study by Orlikowski and Baroudi [2]. However, informed by extant literature on classification of research approaches [29, 28, 35], I for reasons of parsimoniousness employed a reduced version according to the principles of generalizability, empirical fidelity and precision. The methodological approaches employed thereby became survey, case study, and experiment.

3   Methodology

This section first presents the selection of literature and search terms and second describes how the author worked through the selection and classification of the articles that formed the review's body of literature.

3.1   Selection of Literature and Search Terms

Two bodies of literature were selected for review. To ensure high-quality review and a representative body of IS literature [27, 29], eight major IS journals covering the period 2004-2013 were selected: *European Journal of Information System, Information Systems Journal, Information Systems Research, Journal of Association for Information Systems, Journal of Information Technology, Journal of Management Information Systems, Journal of Strategic Information Systems* and *MIS Quarterly*. To complement the established, historical and some could argue conservative body of literature found in these eight major journals, a second body of literature was chosen on the criteria to represent the most current and emerging research in the IS community. In order to fulfill this criteria, the proceedings of finished research from the International Conference on Information Systems (ICIS) 2013 were chosen as adequate.

In order to establish a relevant list of terms for the selection of articles in the subsequent search, I mapped various concepts and definitions of social media. To best possible match the diversity in how social media is predicated, I decided to produce two types of search terms, namely a list of abstract terms and a list consisting of the specific names of relevant social media platforms. The list of abstract terms included 'social media', 'social software', 'social computing', 'social network', 'web 2.0', 'social IT', 'social technology' and 'online community'. The list of specific terms included the most mainstream social network services and rating sites: LinkedIn, MySpace, Facebook, Flickr, YouTube, Twitter, FourSquare, Pinterest, Instagram, Google, Tripadvisor, Trustpilot, and Glassdoor. By using the specific and general search terms in combination, the aim was to find as many relevant articles as possible.

3.2   Selection and Classification of Articles

Out of a total of 2,964 articles published in the eight major IS journals in the period 2004 – 2013, the structured search resulted in a total of 116 articles for which one or more of the search terms were present in the abstract of the article. These 116 articles included both non-empirical research contributions and contributions about social media other than external social media. In order to select the empirical articles and the articles about external social media, I read the abstracts and the methodology section of the papers. The definition of *empirical* research by Mingers [28] was employed. To decide whether an article was about *external* social media, the criteria was that the article explicitly had to describe it as such or its empirical material had to be one on the social media platforms on the list of the specific search terms. This selection process resulted in a total of 42 empirical research contributions about external social media. Concerning the ICIS 2013 proceedings of finished research, I employed an identical search and selection process. This process resulted in a total of 12 articles that were empirical studies of external social media. See column one in table 1 and table 2 to identify the selected articles.

Concerning the classification of the articles with regard to area of research, the review of the two bodies of literature started out by examining the articles according to Avgerou's classification [5]. However, due to a higher analytical adequacy and a more significant pattern regarding actor-focus in the articles, I ended up applying the developed list of potential actors in the field of social media. A number of the articles had a clear actor-focus on individual users or on the user community, but also included aspects of a related organization, and I therefore registered organization as focus-actor in brackets.

In order to examine the articles with regard to conceptual framing and methodology, I read the abstracts and to the extent necessary also the theory and methodology section of the papers. In both bodies of literature three articles clearly differed from the rest by being case based process studies and by the authors furthermore described as employing an interpretive approach. Likewise were three articles among the ICIS 2013 proceedings and 1 article from the eight major journals quickly identified as experiments due to the description of the research setting. Both field and lab experiments were registered as experiments. The remaining articles were categorized as surveys with regard to methodology despite a high diversity in approach. Most probably due to the emerging and diverse nature of digital trace data from user behavior in social media communities, these last-mentioned articles predicated themselves with great variation concerning methodology and data foundation: Empirical survey, archival data, cross-sectional data, etc. Common for all these articles were, however, a quantitative approach and a variance-based conceptualization. Despite the opportunity to differentiate these articles with regard to methodology, this was not done in order to avoid unnecessary blurred boundaries and use of unconventional categories in the classification of the articles.

4   Analysis of IS Literature about Social Media

This section presents the analysis of the two bodies of empirical IS literature about external social media. First, the analysis of the selected articles from the eight major IS journals in the period 2004–2013 is presented. Second, the analysis of the finished research proceedings from ICIS 2013 is presented.

4.1   Analysis of Eight Major IS Journals 2004-2013

The most striking finding in the analysis of research area in the articles from the eight major journals, relates to the actors that are in focus of the studies. The analysis shows an almost total dominance of focus on users behavior in extant IS literature about social media. Out of 42 articles, 40 articles focus on user behavior. Two articles have their primary focus on technology vendors. The analysis found no indication of articles in the eight major journals that had the behavior of organizations, consultancies or media as their primary focus. A detailed examination of the articles shows that 4 articles indirectly include the behavior of the firm and one article includes an analytical glance at the technology vendor. However, it is the users point of view that establishes the perspective for including these other actors in the field of social media.

Concerning conceptual framing in the eight major journals, the analysis point to dominance of variance studies. Three articles conduct a process study whereas the rest of the articles epistemologically are framed as variance studies.

Concerning the methodological approach, the detected pattern shows 38 survey, 3 case studies and 1 experiment. See table 1 for an overview of the analysis.

Table 1. Analysis of eight major IS journals 2004-2013 about social media

	Research area					Framework		Methodology		
	User community	Technology vendor	Organization	Consultancies	Media	Variance study	Process study	Survey	Case study	Experiment
Bateman et al. 2011 [36]	X					X		X		
Campbell et al. 2009 [37]	X						X		X	
Chau and Xu 2012 [38]	X					X		X		
Cheng et al. 2011 [39]	X					X		X		
Claussen et al. 2013 [40]		X				X		X		
Dewan and Ramaprasad 2012 [41]	X					X		X		
Garg et al 2011 [42]	X					X		X		
Germonprez and Hovorka 2013 [43]	X	(X)					X		X	
Gnyawali et al. 2010 [44]		X				X		X		
Goh et al. 2013 [45]	X		(X)			X		X		
Khan and Jarvenpaa 2010 [46]	X					X		X		
Krasnova et al. 2010 [47]	X					X		X		
Luo et al. 2013 [48]	X		(X)			X		X		
Miller and Tucker 2013 [49]	X		(X)			X		X		
Moser et al. 2013 [50]	X					X		X		
Oestreicher and Zalmanson 2013 [51]	X					X		X		
Oh et al. 2013 [52]	X					X		X		
Posey et al. 2010 [53]	X					X		X		
Ransbotham and Kane 2011 [54]	X					X		X		
Ren et al. 2012 [55]	X					X				X
Rishika et al. 2013 [56]	X		(X)			X				
Shi and Whinston 2013 [57]	X					X		X		
Silva et al. 2008 [58]	X						X		X	
Stieglitz and Dang-Xuan 2013 [59]	X					X		X		
Susarla et al. 2013 [60]	X					X		X		
Tang et al. 2012 [61]	X					X		X		
Tow et al. 2010 [62]	X					X		X		
Wattal et al. 2010 [63]	X					X		X		
Xin Xu and Zhang 2013 [64]	X					X		X		
Xu et al. 2011 [65]	X					X		X		
Zeng and Wei 2013 [66]	X					X		X		
Zhang and Watts 2008 [67]	X					X		X		

4.2   Analysis of Proceedings from ICIS 2013

Similar to the analysis of the eight major journals, the proceedings from ICIS 2013 show dominance of articles that focus on user behavior. Out of 12 articles, 11 articles focus on user behavior. 1 article focuses on an organization's use of social media. Concerning conceptual framing and especially methodology, the proceedings show a relative higher variation. Out of the 12 articles, 9 articles are variance studies while 3 articles are process studies. Concerning the methodological approach, 6 are surveys, 3 are case studies, and 3 are experiments. With regard to framework and methodology, the ICIS proceedings therefore have a relatively higher variation than the articles from the eight major journals. See table 2 for an overview of the analysis.

Table 2. Analysis of ECIS 2013 proceedings about social media

	Research area					Framework		Methodology		
	User community	Technology vendor	Organization	Consultancies	Media	Variance study	Process study	Survey	Case study	Experiment
Burtch et al. 2013 [68]	X					X		X		
Dhillon and Chowdhuri 2013 [69]	X					X		X		
Eling et al. 2013 [70]	X					X				X
Freeman et al. 2013 [71]	X						X		X	
Heath et al. 2013 [72]		X					X		X	
Hill et al. 2013 [73]	X					X		X		
Oh et al. 2013 [74]	X					X				X
Siering and Muntermann 2013 [75]	X					X		X		
Shi et al. 2013 [76]	X					X				X
Tan and Tan 2013 [77]	X						X		X	
Velichety and Ram 2013 [78]	X					X		X		
Zhu et al. 2013 [79]	X					X		X		

5   Discussion and Future Agenda

This section discusses the review findings and suggests two main priorities for future IS research. The section is finalized by recognizing the limitations of the review and by explaining the suggested dialectical approach as one of wrestling.

5.1   Organizational Use of Social Media

The review of the two bodies of IS literature indicated a dominance of user-focused research about social media. The IS discipline thereby mirrors a strong user-paradigm in the disciplines of innovation management and marketing [6, 8]. In order to differentiate the IS discipline, I suggest IS scholars to draw on home ground advantages. This and the following paragraph will sketch possible first tentative steps in such a process.

To strengthen future research, an inclusion of all relevant actors in the field will contribute to a differentiated understanding of social media. However, in order to specifically strengthen IS research in the interdisciplinary field of research about social media, the paper suggest IS scholars to draw on the history of the IS discipline as a groundswell of knowledge, and therefore to prioritize organizational use of social media as their home ground.

Avgerou's classification of IS research [5] can direct such studies and anchor them in extant IS literature. A couple of examples can illustrate the suggested approach. For the area 'the process of systems development' we can draw on studies of innovation of digital infrastructure [21] and for the area 'information systems management' one possible path is to draw on IS studies of outsourcing [80] to investigate the widespread outsourcing of social media. In relation to the area 'the societal impact of information systems', studies of accountability [83] already has established a solid starting point. Figure 1 illustrates a translation of the original research areas with regard to organizational use of social media and a potential IS article as starting point. The original classification of IS research can thereby facilitate systematically directed studies of social media on IS home ground.

Classification of IS research	Organizational use of social media	IS article starting point
Applications of IT to support the functioning of an organization.	Coupling of social media to the functioning of an organization.	Yoo et al 2010 [83]
The process of systems development.	Development of social media in a context of digital infrastructure.	Tilson et al 2010 [21]
Information systems management	Organizations' management of social media generativity.	Jarvenpaa and Tuunainen 2013 [22]
The organizational value of information systems.	Social media contribution to value creation in organizations.	Avgerou 2000 [84]
The societal impact of information systems.	Impact of organizations' interaction with social media on society.	Orlikowski and Barley 2001 [85].

Fig. 1. IS home ground areas for future study of social media

5.2   Multi Stage Process Studies

The analysis of extant IS literature about social media detected a dominance of survey based variance studies. In order to complement this epistemology it is therefore suggested to prioritize case based process studies [34]. The IS discipline has always had been a strong focus on the intricate interaction between organizations and IT, and how it develops over time and on different levels of organizing [85]. A seminal article that draws on structuration theory [86] can function as starting point for studying how todays organizations interact with social media. IS studies that draw on institutional theory with a multi stage lens [32] can emphasize how development is not necessarily a linear process and how the technological artifact changes during the process [87] or is loosely coupled to the change process [84]. Figure 2 illustrates a multi stage process model aimed at describing organizational interaction with social media. The model is adapted from a combination of seminal IS literature [86] and recent institutional theory [32]. The graphics in second row illustrates the type of relation between the involved actors: Constellation, conflict and convergence.

Stage 1	Stage 2	Stage 3
Initial development	Initial use	Ongoing use

Fig. 2. Multi stage process model for organizational use of social media

5.3   Limitations and Wrestling

The review has a number of limitations. The classification of the articles according to the categories in the three dimensions was not a straightforward and just practical procedure as also pointed in earlier examinations of IS research [28]. Especially the classification of the articles with regard to methodology indicated need for differentiation and terminological clarification in perspective of the emerging forms of digital trace data in the field of social media. This may include both technical [88] and ethical [89] issues. The classification of the articles with regard to research area indicated a number of articles that focused on user behavior, but also indirectly included organizational use of social media, and thereby pointed to the relevance of a more differentiated analytical grid.

To further validate the examination of extant IS literature about social media with regard to research approaches, it is therefore suggested to develop a more differentiated scheme of classification as well as to employ an inter coder procedure as part of the examination.

This review of past literature and to prepare future research [27] is understood as a dialectical [90] development process. However, as the difference between the review findings and the suggested agenda indicates, this development is understood less as a progression than an continued wrestling with contradictions on IS home ground [5].

References

1. Markus, M.L., Robey, D.: Information Technology and Organizational Change: Causal Structure in Theory and Research. Manage. Sci. 34, 583–599 (1988)
2. Orlikovski, W.J., Baroudi, J.J.: Studying Information Technology in Organizations: Research Approaches and Assumptions. Inf. Syst. Res. 2, 1–28 (1991)
3. Chiasson, M., Germonprez, M., Mathiassen, L.: Pluralist action research: a review of the information systems literature. Inf. Syst. J. 19, 31–54 (2009)
4. Mathiassen, L., Chiasson, M., Germonprez, M.: Style Composition in Action Research Publication (2012)
5. Avgerou, C.: Information systems: what sort of science is it? Omega 28, 567–579 (2000)

6. Baldwin, C., von Hippel, E.: Modeling a Paradigm Shift: From Producer Innovation to User and Open Collaborative Innovation (2011)
7. Lakhani, K.R., von Hippel, E.: How open source software works: "free" user-to-user assistance. Res. Policy. 32, 923–943 (2003)
8. Dellarocas, C.: The Digitization of Word of Mouth: Promise and Challenges of Online Feedback Mechanisms. Manage. Sci. 49, 1407–1424 (2003)
9. Godes, D., Mayzlin, D., Chen, Y., Das, S., Dellarocas, C., Pfeiffer, B., Libai, B., Sen, S., Shi, M., Verlegh, P.: The Firm's Management of Social Interactions. Mark. Lett. 16, 415–428 (2005)
10. Macnamara, J., Zerfass, A.: Social Media Communication in Organizations: The Challenges of Balancing Openness, Strategy, and Management. Int. J. Strateg. Commun. 6, 287–308 (2012)
11. Zerfass, A., Fink, S., Linke, A.: Social media governance: Regulartory frameworks as drivers of succes in online communications (2011)
12. Zammuto, R.F., Griffith, T.L., Majchrzak, A., Dougherty, D.J., Faraj, S.: Information Technology and the Changing Fabric of Organization. Organ. Sci. 18, 749–762 (2007)
13. Aakhus, M.: Information systems for symbolic action: social media and beyond. MIS Q. (2012)
14. Armstrong, A., Hagel III, J.: The Real Value of ON-LINE Communities. Harv. Bus. Rev. 74, 134–141 (1996)
15. Paramewaran, M., Whinston, A.: Research issues in social computing. J. Assoc. Inf. Syst. 8 (2007)
16. Merali, Y., Papadopoulos, T., Nadkarni, T.: Information systems strategy: Past, present, future? J. Strateg. Inf. Syst. 21, 125–153 (2012)
17. Stenmark, D.: Web 2.0 in the Business Environment: The New Intranet or a Passing Hype? In: Proceedings of the 16th European Conference on Information Systems, ECIS 2008 (2008)
18. Bergquist, A. E.: Social Media as Management Fashion - A Discourse Perspective. In: The 21st European Conference on Information Systems (2013)
19. Baskervillle, R., Myers, M.D.: Fashion Waves in Information Systems Research and Practice. MIS Q. 33, 647–662 (2009)
20. Wang, P.: Chasing the Hottest IT: Effects of Information Technology Fashion on Organizations. MIS Q. 34, 63–85 (2010)
21. Tilson, D., Lyytinen, K., Sørensen, C.: Digital Infrastructures: The Missing IS Research Agenda. Inf. Syst. Res. 21, 748–759 (2010)
22. Jarvenpaa, S.L., Tuunainen, V.K.: Theoretical Elaboration of IT Enablement Model in the Era of Customer and Community Digital Innovation. In: 21st European Conference on Information Systems (2013)
23. Jarvenpaa, S.L., Staples, D.S.: The use of collaborative electronic media for information sharing: an exploratory study of determinants. J. Strateg. Inf. Syst. 9, 129–154 (2000)
24. Star, S.L., Ruhleder, K.: Steps Toward an Ecology of Infrastructure: Design and Access for Large Information Spaces. Inf. Syst. Res. 7, 111–134 (1996)
25. Haefliger, S., Monteiro, E., Foray, D., von Krogh, G.: Social Software and Strategy. Long Range Plann. 44, 297–316 (2011)
26. von Krogh, G.: How does social software change knowledge management? Toward a strategic research agenda. J. Strateg. Inf. Syst., 154–164 (2012)
27. Webster, J., Watson, R.: Analyzing the Past to Prepare for the Future: Writing a Literature Review. MIS Q. 26 (2002)
28. Mingers, J.: The paucity of multimethod research: a review of the information systems literature. Inf. Syst. J. 13, 233–249 (2003)

29. Chen, W., Hirschheim, R.: A paradigmatic and methodological examination of information systems research from 1991 to 2001. Inf. Syst. J. 14, 197–235 (2004)
30. Aral, S., Dellarocas, C., Godes, D.: Social Media and Business Transformation: A Framework for Research. Inf. Syst. Res. 24, 3–13 (2013)
31. Dimaggio, P.J., Powell, W.W.: The Iron Cage Revisited: Institutional Isomorphism and Collective Rationality in Organizational Fields. Am. Sociol. Rev. 48, 147–160 (1983)
32. Colyvas, J.A., Powell, W.W.: Roads to Institutionalization: The Remaking of Boundaries Between Public and Private Science. Res. Organ. Behav. 27, 305–353 (2006)
33. Haahr, L.: Exploratory Framework for Organizations as Actors on Facebook. Working paper, 35th IRIS Seminar, Stockholm, Sweden, pp. 1–15 (2012)
34. Poole, M.S., Van de Ven, A.H.: Alternative Approaches for Studying Organizational Change. Organ. Stud. 26, 1377–1404 (2005)
35. Van De Ven, A.H.: Engaged Scholarship. A guide for organizational and social research. Oxfor University Press (2007)
36. Bateman, P.J., Gray, P.H., Butler, B.S.: The Impact of Community Commitment on Participation in Online Communities. Inf. Syst. Res. 22, 841–854 (2011)
37. Campbell, J., Fletcher, G., Greenhill, A.: Conflict and identity shape shifting in an online financial community. Inf. Syst. J. 19, 461–478 (2009)
38. Chau, M., Xu, J.: Business Intelligence in Blogs: Understanding Consumer Interactions and Communities. MIS Q. 36, 1189–1216 (2012)
39. Cheng, J., Sun, A., Hu, D., Zeng, D.: An Information Diffusion-Based Recommendation Framework for Micro-Blogging. J. Assoc. Inf. Syst. 12, 463–486 (2011)
40. Claussen, J., Kretschmer, T., Mayrhofer, P.: The Effects of Rewarding User Engagement: The Case of Facebook Apps. Inf. Syst. Res. 24, 186–200 (2013)
41. Dewan, S., Ramaprasad, J.: Music Blogging, Online Sampling, and the Long Tail. Inf. Syst. Res. 23, 1056–1067 (2012)
42. Garg, R., Smith, M.D., Telang, R.: Measuring Information Diffusion in an Online Community. J. Manag. Inf. Syst. 28, 11–38 (2011)
43. Germonprez, M., Hovorka, D.S.: Member engagement within digitally enabled social network communities: new methodological considerations. Inf. Syst. J. 23, 525–549 (2013)
44. Gnyawali, D.R., Fan, W., Penner, J.: Competitive Actions and Dynamics in the Digital Age: An Empirical Investigation of Social Networking Firms. Inf. Syst. Res. 21, 594–613 (2010)
45. Goh, K.-Y., Heng, C.-S., Lin, Z.: Social Media Brand Community and Consumer Behavior: Quantifying the Relative Impact of User- and Marketer-Generated Content. Inf. Syst. Res. 24, 88–107 (2013)
46. Khan, Z., Jarvenpaa, S.L.: Exploring temporal coordination of events with Facebook.com. J. Inf. Technol (Palgrave Macmillan) 25, 137–151 (2010)
47. Krasnova, H., Spiekermann, S., Koroleva, K., Hildebrand, T.: Online social networks: why we disclose. J. Inf. Technol (Palgrave Macmillan) 25, 109–125 (2010)
48. Luo, X., Zhang, J., Duan, W.: Social Media and Firm Equity Value. Inf. Syst. Res. 24, 146–163 (2013)
49. Miller, A.R., Tucker, C.: Active Social Media Management: The Case of Health Care. Inf. Syst. Res. 24, 52–70 (2013)
50. Moser, C., Ganley, D., Groenewegen, P.: Communicative genres as organising structures in online communities - of team players and storytellers. Inf. Syst. J. 23, 551–567 (2013)
51. Oestreicher-Singer, G., Zalmanson, L.: Content or Community? A Digital Business Strategy for Content Providers in the Social Age. MIS Q. 37, 591–616 (2013)
52. Oh, O., Agrawal, M., Rao, H.R.: Community Intelligence and Social Media Services: A Rumor theoretical Analysis of Tweets During Social Crises. MIS Q. 37, 407–A7 (2013)

53. Posey, C., Lowry, P.B., Roberts, T.L., Ellis, T.S.: Proposing the online community self-disclosure model: the case of working professionals in France and the U.K. who use online communities. Eur. J. Inf. Syst. 19, 181–195 (2010)

54. Ransbotham, S., Kane, G.C.: Membership Turnover and Collaboration Succes in Online Communities: Explaining Rises and Falls from Grace in Wikipedia. MIS Q. 35, 613–627 (2011)

55. Ren, Y., Harper, F.M., Drenner, S., Terveen, L., Kiesler, S., Riedl, J., Kraut, R.E.: Building Member Attachment in Online Communities: Applying Theories of group Identity and Interpersonal Bonds. MIS Q. 36, 841–864 (2012)

56. Rishika, R., Kumar, A., Janakiraman, R., Bezawada, R.: The Effect of Customers' Social Media Participation on Customer Visit Frequency and Profitability: An Empirical Investigation. Inf. Syst. Res. 24, 108–127 (2013)

57. Shi, Z., Whinston, A.B.: Network Structure and Observational Learning: Evidence from a Location-Based Social Network. J. Manag. Inf. Syst. 30, 185–212 (2013)

58. Silva, L., Goel, L., Mousavidin, E.: Exploring the dynamics of blog communities: the case of MetaFilter. Inf. Syst. J. 19, 55–81 (2009)

59. Stieglitz, S., Dang-Xuan, L.: Emotions and Information Diffusion in Social Media-Sentiment of Microblogs and Sharing Behavior. J. Manag. Inf. Syst. 29, 217–248 (2013)

60. Susarla, A., Oh, J.-H., Tan, Y.: Social Networks and the Diffusion of User-Generated Content: Evidence from YouTube. Inf. Syst. Res. 23, 23–41 (2012)

61. Tang, Q., Gu, B., Whinston, A.B.: Content Contribution for Revenue Sharing and Reputation in Social Media: A Dynamic Structural Model. J. Manag. Inf. Syst. 29, 41–76 (2012)

62. Tow, W.N.-F.H., Dell, P., Venable, J.: Understanding information disclosure behaviour in Australian Facebook users. J. Inf. Technol. (Palgrave Macmillan) 25, 126–136 (2010)

63. Wattal, S., Schuff, D., Mandviwalla, M., Williams, C.B.: Web 2.0 and Politics: The 2008 U.S. Presidential Election and an E-Politics Research Agenda. MIS Q. 34, 669–688 (2010)

64. Xin Xu, S., Zhang, X. (Michael): Impact of Wikipedia on Market Information Environment: Evidence on Management Disclosure and Investor Reaction. MIS Q. 37, 1043–A10 (2013)

65. Xu, H., Dinev, T., Smith, J., Hart, P.: Information Privacy Concerns: Linking Individual Perceptions with Institutional Privacy Assurances. J. Assoc. Inf. Syst. 12, 798–824 (2011)

66. Zeng, X., Wei, L.: Social Ties and User Content Generation: Evidence from Flickr. Inf. Syst. Res. 24, 71–87 (2013)

67. Zhang, W., Watts, S.A.: Capitalizing on Content: Information Adoption in Two Online communities. J. Assoc. Inf. Syst. 9, 72–93 (2008)

68. Burtch, G., Ghose, A., Wattal, S.: An Empirical Examination of Users ' Information Hiding in a Crowdfunding Context. In: Thirty Fourth International Conference on Information Systems, Milan 2013, pp. 1–19 (2013)

69. Dhillon, G., Chowdhuri, R.: Individual Values for Protecting Identity in Social Networks. In: Thirty Fourth International Conference on Information Systems, Milan 2013, pp. 1–16 (2013)

70. Eling, N., Widjaja, T., Krasnova, H., Buxmann, P.: Will You Accept an App? Emperical Investigation of the Desicional Calculus Behind the Adoption of Applications on Facebook. In: Thirty Fourth International Conference on Information Systems, Milan 2013, pp. 1–20 (2013)

71. Freeman, M.B., Halliwell, M., Freeman, A.: Social Media Influence on Viewer Engagement. In: Thirty Fourth International Conference on Information Systems, Milan 2013, pp. 1–16 (2013)

72. Heath, D., Kroll-Smith, S., Ganesh, J., Singh, R.: Exploring Strategic Organizational Engagement in Social Media: A Revelatory Case. In: Thirty Fourth International Conference on Information Systems, Milan 2013, pp. 1–15 (2013)

73. Hill, S., Benton, A., Van den Bulte, C.: When Does Social Network-Based Prediction Work? A Large Scale Analysis of Brand and TV Audience Engagement by Twitter Users. In: Thirty Fourth International Conference on Information Systems, Milan 2013, pp. 1–16 (2013)

74. Oh, H., Animesh, A., Pinsonneault, A.: Free vs. For a Fee: The Impact of Information Pricing Strategy on the Pattern and Effectiveness of Word-of-Mouth via Social Media. In: Thirty Fourth International Conference on Information Systems, Milan 2013, pp. 1–18 (2013)

75. Siering, M., Muntermann, J.: How to Identify Tomorrow's Most Active Social Commerce Contributors? Inviting Starlets to the Reviewer Hall of Fame. In: Thirty Fourth International Conference on Information Systems, Milan 2013, pp. 1–18 (2013)

76. Shi, N., Wang, K., Hong, K.Y., Pavlou, P.A.: Social Commers Beyond Word of Mouth: Role of Social Distance and Social Norms in Online Refferal Incentive Systems. In: Thirty Fourth International Conference on Information Systems, Milan (2013)

77. Tan, B., Tan, F.T.C.: Nurturing and Leveraging Virtual Communities: A Two-Dimensional Process Model. In: Thirty Fourth International Conference on Information Systems, Milan 2013, pp. 1–20 (2013)

78. Velichety, S., Ram, S.: A Cross-Sectional and Temporal Analysis of Information Consumption on Twitter. In: Thirty Fourth International Conference on Information Systems, Milan 2013, pp. 1–18 (2013)

79. Zhu, H., Kraut, R.E., Kittur, A.: The Impact of Membership Overlap on the Survival of Online Communities. In: Thirty Fourth International Conference on Information Systems, Milan 2013, pp. 1–17 (2013)

80. Chang, Y.B., Gurbaxani, V.: Information Technology Outsourcing, Knowledge Transfer, and Firm Productivity: An Empirical Analysis. MIS Q. 36, 1043–1063 (2012)

81. Scott, S., Orlikowski, W.: Getting the Truth: Exploring the Material Grounds of Institutional Dynamics in Social Media. Pap. Submitt. to EGOS 2009 Sub-theme 08 — Institutions Knowl. Role Mater. (2009)

82. Scott, S.V., Orlikowski, W.J.: Reconfiguring relations of accountability: Materialization of social media in the travel sector. Accounting, Organ. Soc. 37, 26–40 (2012)

83. Yoo, Y., Henfridsson, O., Lyytinen, K.: The New Organizing Logic of Digital Innovation: An Agenda for Information Systems Research (2010)

84. Avgerou, C.: IT and organizational change: an institutionalist perspective. Inf. Technol. People. 13, 234–262 (2000)

85. Orlikowski, W.J., Barley, S.R.: Technology and Institutions: What can Reserach on Information Technology and Research on Organizations Learn from Each Other? MIS Q. 25, 145–165 (2001)

86. Orlikowski, W.J.: The Duality of Technology: Rethinking the Concept of Technology in Organizations. Organ. Sci. 3, 398–427 (1992)

87. Currie, W.L.: The organizing vision of application service provision: a process-oriented analysis. Inf. Organ. 14, 237–267 (2004)

88. Howison, J., Wiggins, A., Crowston, K.: Validity Issues in the Use of Social Network Analysis with Digital Trace Data. J. Assoc. Inf. Syst. 12, 767–797 (2011)

89. Schultze, U., Mason, R.O.: Studying cyborgs: re-examining internet studies as human subjects research. J. Inf. Technol. (Palgrave Macmillan) 27, 301–312 (2012)

90. Benson, J.K.: Organizations: A Dialectical View. Adm. Sci. Q. 22, 1–21 (1977)

Designing Scientific Creativity

Erik Kristiansen[1], Jan Pries-Heje[1], and Richard L. Baskerville[2]

[1] Department of Communication, Business, and Information Technologies,
Roskilde University, Universitetsvej 1, Postboks 260, 4000 Roskilde, Denmark
[2] Department of Computer Information Systems, Georgia State University,
Post Office Box 4015, Atlanta, Georgia 30302-4015, USA
{erikk,janph}@ruc.dk, baskerville@acm.org

Abstract. On one hand, information systems design demands the creativity of art; on the other, it demands the methodical rigor of science. An emphasis on design rigor can diminish our attention on design creativity. In this paper, we explore the relationship between the creative and the methodical aspects of design, and propose a novel, generic design approach that invokes creativity by provoking divergent thinking and context in the design processes while retaining the analytical and methodical aspects. Using design science research, we study the utility of this generic design approach by using it to develop a game design method named site-storming. From this specific case of a design method we explore if we can design an explanatory design theory of scientific creativity. Our results show that creativity and science may coexist in a creativity method, but that the method only delivers, if they are balanced correctly.

Keywords: creativity, design method, design science, explanatory design theory.

1   Introduction

The Danish Nature Agency and GeoCenter Møns Klint wanted to engage children aged 12-15 in a physical exploration of the nature area around the famous chalk cliffs of Møn (Denmark), which include dense forest, steep hills and views over the tall chalk cliffs a hundred meters down to the sea. The museum at the cliffs tells the story of the natural development of the cliffs and the present flora and fauna unique to the area. The museum combines exhibitions inside the museum building with guided tours of the local environment. The museum also operates an educational section which focuses on educational programs for visiting school classes.

The GeoCenter believed a computer supported outdoor game could be used in conjunction with the educational program in order to promote on-site learning about the area. While still lacking a well-defined set of requirements other than a general idea of a game, a development team set out to design a site-specific or pervasive computer game. Because no available methodical approach fit, the team proceeded with generative design-oriented project work as a series of unstructured experiments

T.H. Commisso et al. (Eds.): SCIS 2014, LNBIP 186, pp. 44–57, 2014.

using prototyping. However the first prototype failed and called for a more structured approach, which in turn raised methodological questions. Would a more structured approach ensure a successful game and a successful project, or would it crush the creativity that makes a game fun? How can we add some rigorous features of science (such as methodical, logical, reliable, and repeatable) to a creative task without diminishing the creativity? This led to the research question addressed in this paper: How can we "balance" creativity and science in information systems design settings? By this question we set out to explore if we can design an explanatory design theory based on both structure (some of the rigorous features of science) and creativity. We follow the epistemology of utility rather than truth [27], as our case is a game-design method, that when properly used, should produce games that are of value to the designers (the game designers) by being of value to the users (the players). It is however difficult to assess whether a creativity method is of any value, because we do not know the precise connection between the outcome of the method and the evaluation of the players. We assume that a design method is of value, if the designers using it, express that the method furthers their design work. This must be considered highly subjective, and is another argument for introducing structures in the creativity process that make it more scientific and less subjective. We studied the value of the method by evaluating both the designers and users in activity, by using qualitative methods. We use the word "balance" to indicate that we want to combine creativity and science, but we do not know how much science "equals" how much creativity, if this at all gives meaning. We assume that a certain "balance" is achieved if we succeed in including both creativity and science, and that the resulting design method meets with approval from the designers.

The remainder of this paper is structured as follows. In section 2 we review the literature on science and creativity in design. In section 3, we describe the design science research approach used to study the problem. In section 4 we design a generic approach to enhancing creativity in design science. Then in section 5 we specifically apply this approach to the Cliffs of Møn problem. In section 6, we detail the evaluation of the specific application of the approach, finding a good balance between creativity and structure. We elaborate on that conclusion and identify an explanatory design theory with the elements of the generic approach in section 7. Section 8 concludes the paper and discusses further research.

2 Science and Creativity in Design

Science and creativity may seem to be notions from different academic fields. Yet creative design is found in many logical, methodical arenas such as engineering, medicine and architecture. Creativity is not just a property connected to psychology, the arts, and cognitive science. But the struggle in finding a reasonable balance between structure and creativity plays out in information systems along with other logical and methodical arenas. In this section we survey the essential background literature necessary before exploring how information systems design can better embrace creativity.

2.1 Creativity

"Creativity" has very positive connotations, coming to us directly from the Latin *Creare*, which means to create. Amabile [1] describes creativity as a function of three components: expertise, motivation and creative-thinking skills, where expertise and creative thinking skills are regarded as individuals' natural resources. In practice creativity is also related to the distinction between divergent and convergent thinking [24], [25]. Divergent thinking about a problem requires creativity to open up multiple ways to solve the problem. Convergent thinking requires analytic and logical thinking to close in on the best solution to a problem. Some scholars recommend the use of divergent thinking at the 'fuzzy' front-end [32], [46], while others recommend more flexible use of divergent thinking during the design process [37].

2.2 Creativity and Design Method

It is important to recognizing the interaction between creativity and design method. An important concept in this interaction is *fixation* [28], [45]. Fixation is a premature commitment to design solutions based on previous knowledge, emotions, metaphors or social relationships [36]. Fixation affects the generation of alternatives, knowledge acquisition, collaborative creativity, and creativity processes. These effects lead to a lack of creativity in a design practice. Such uncreative designs ultimately result in inadequate products that are fine targets for new design theories. The theories result in new models of thought to deal with inadequate products. This may lead to new fixations that may need to be addressed by further creative work [36].

Early work in design method favored scientific problem-solving in the 1960s [3], [52]. As this work matured, the strict methodological approach was rejected in the 1970s by some of its earlier proponents (e.g., leading design scientists Christopher Alexander and J. Christopher Jones, see [14]. This was partly due to the fact that some design methods were not able to address 'wicked' problems as opposed to the 'tame' problems that had been more easily addressed by the techniques of science and engineering [47]. These critics observe that Simon's design science and the other older design methods based on problem solving are unable to address creativity issues [21], [26]. It is a dilemma that embodies a struggle between structure and creativity. This dilemma asks, do design methods and design theory defeat creativity or does creativity defeat design methods [36]? This potentially contradictory relationship builds on three issues (ibid.): (1) awareness and control over fixation, (2) reliance on convergence or divergence or both, (3) the degree of autonomy versus control in the design organization. Design methods devise combinations of these parameters, e.g. divergence before convergence, awareness and avoidance of fixation, and increasing creativity by control over the design process. While creativity and structure are both necessary in the design process, these are unlikely bedfellows, and each tends to limit the possibilities of the other.

3   Research Method

To answer the research question on how we can balance creativity and structure we need a research method. A quantitative method is out of the question as not enough people worked on this problem. A descriptive study would require us to be able to find some designers trying to balance creativity and structure, which we are unable to. That leaves us with an action or design oriented approach. Hence we decided to undertake an action case study developing an explanatory design theory.

An *action case* study is a variant of action research focusing on interpretation of the case. It combines intervention and interpretation in order to achieve both change and understanding. We found it to be a perfect way of working through a number of iterations with our research question. In each iteration we then try to interpret the outcome in the form an explanatory design theory.

An *explanatory design theory* [7] provides a functional explanation as to why a solution has certain components in terms of the requirements stated in the design. The main requirement in our research question is to be able to balance structure and creativity. The main components of a solution will be the answer to *how* to balance? What we look for then – when interpreting the action case – is functional explanations of how to balance structure and creativity.

We have adopted *Design Science Research* (DSR) as research framework for our study because it strives for both rigor and relevance. In our search for design science rigor, and our focus on the practical problem, the creative and innovative aspect, which is less structured, is easily ignored. DSR has gained an increasing presence in the field of information systems [44] that is capturing the field's increasing attention to the importance of the IS artifact [40] and its relevance to practice [58].

In the DSR study below, our integration of structure, rigor and creativity aimed symbiotically at a solution to the problem at hand, a more generic approach for broader use, and at a specific approach for the setting. As a result, there were three products in this study. The *design science product* is the generic approach. The *design product* in this study is the specific method used for designing a game. The third product was a game (an IT artifact) that was designed and evaluated using the specific method.

Against this complex backdrop of design creativity, method, and science, we set out to investigate the balance of the three elements in the context of the design problem at GeoCenter Møn.

4   Designing a Generic Approach

The first condition to avoid in designing a creative design approach is fixation (as discussed above). Fixation arises because *humans think traditionally unless otherwise provoked*. Edward de Bono [16], [17], [18] notes that all self-organizing systems form such patterns or habits, and creativity arises from thinking differently, or moving across these patterns instead of just following them. Such *Lateral Thinking* is necessary change one's starting point and perception of how things connect, thinking in a fundamentally different way.

4.1 Provoking Untraditional Thinking

Divergent thinking generates a variety of ideas linked to a problem or concept; it involves free association and broad scanning ability [48]. Because play has been shown to facilitate divergent thinking [53], we use play as a component in a process that can provoke or spur untraditional thinking and creativity.

In addition, we adapted "card" concepts from IDEO [10], [30], [31]. An approach used to strategize innovation in the design of products, spaces, services and experiences. IDEO derives insights from understanding people and their experiences, behaviors, perceptions and needs. It uses Method Cards that can help a team to obtain new creative insights [8].

4.2 Accommodate the Situation

Given the centrality of creativity, enforcing a common solution structure is contradictory to our purpose. The *context* of the method's usage must be allowed to have its impact on the artifact. Among the different important properties of context to consider are cognitive, social, cultural, and physical [35]. Design practice as a *situation* is also described in [54], where creativity is regarded a dynamic and situated process aimed at a broader social context.

In the case of the Cliffs of Møn the place of the game performance is part of the artifact. This suggests in itself that the context should not only be explored, but the principle requires the context to be an intrinsic part of the performance of the design method. The context in which the design work is performed has a definite impact on creativity [2], [41].

Accordingly, there is a general requirement that designers make *accommodations for the physical environment* in which the designed artifact will operate. In Simon's terms, this is the external interface design of the artifact, such that the environment and the artifact match according to the purpose at hand. For the purpose of our generic approach, it means matching the IS design to the constraints and affordances that are delivered intrinsically by the physical site in which the IS users will operate. In terms of design theory, this requirement embodies a specific capability of designers. That is, designers must be able to accommodate the physical environment.

4.3 Have Fun

Humans are attracted to fun; an important condition related to creativity, different ways of thinking, and untraditional thinking. Promoting the pleasure that designers obtain from the design process is likely to promote fun and pleasure in the ultimate user operation of the artifact. Not surprisingly creativity and play have often been linked in research. This linkage is particularly the case for types of play such as "mimicry" [11], "make-believe play" [51], "play as the imaginary" [55] and "pretend play", which are regarded as facilitators of creative processes [22], [49], [53]. This facilitation arises because the nature of play is understood as "doing something not for real." Theoretical research has described play as fostering the development of affective and cognitive processes that are regarded important for the creative process and the creative product, and that play actually facilitates creativity [50]. This facilitating is also supported by a study showing that motivation based on "fun" affects performance in a positive way when performing a task [6]. The design process itself can be based on fun, by designing the method as a game.

4.4   Combine Individual and Group Work

We also adapted the concept from group decision making (cf. [43]) that *combining individual and group work* stimulates more ideas in general and more creative ideas in particular; specifically in relation to the amount of time committed to the design process by the designers. In the generic approach we take into account that more ideas for the time invested are brought forward if the structure provides a good way to combine individual and group work. The approach strikes a balance between structure and creativity where the structure intends to promote creativity rather than inhibit it.

5   Designing a Specific Approach

Based on the general requirements described in section 4, we designed a specific approach, the *site-storming method* that embodies each of the principles. It is an idea-generation method for outdoor computer games (the genre called *pervasive games* or *site-specific games* (cf. [33], [39]). The artifacts produced by the design method are game concepts.

5.1   Untraditional Thinking

The design process provokes creativity by using the structure of a *design-game* to force divergent thinking. In this way, the game designer works out the design in a form of meta-game: the design-game played in order to design the *instance-game* (the designed artifact). The design-game uses two strategies: design-game cards and a performative approach to playing the design-game. The game deck consists of 56 cards in three categories: 32 mission cards, 16 game-type cards and 8 prop cards. All the cards are double the size of ordinary playing cards (equal to the paper format A6), but still easy to carry along. On the back of each mission card there is a picture of a playful situation for further inspiration. The mission cards provide a suggested name of the game (the instance-game), a one-liner for inspiration, what the designer has to explore, some questions the designer should think about, and finally an instruction to communicate the experiences of the design session into a game. The mission cards are inspired by psychogeography [13] and the titles listed in Table 1 suggest their content.

Table 1. Design-Game Card Names

Mission Cards	Game Type Cards	Prop Cards
Strange Tags	The Spectacular Game	SMS
Time Travel		
Mapping the Game	Conspiracy Game	Bluetooth
Another Place		
Writing the Streets	The Disruptive Game	No-tech Props
Subverting Cartography		
The Swarm	Item Hunt Game	Tags
All Roads Lead to Rome		
There is no … Escape	Strategy Game	Camera
Darkness in the Market Place		
Tagging the City	Role-Playing Game	Costume
Impossible Links		
Hidden Secrets	Puzzle Game	Street Art
Where Will I Go?		
Tell Me More	Pick And Deliver Game	Searching Equipment
The Color Conquest		
Secret Meetings	Memory Game	
Routes Uncovered		
Space Explored	The Props Game	
The Social Game		
Repressed Desires	Trading Game	
Follow Me		
Personal Performances	The Construction Game	
Unsolved Mystery		
Architecture	The Performative Game	
The Algorithmic Walk		
In-Between Spaces	Maze Game	
Forbidden Spaces		
Where Am I?	Stealth Game	
Keep Away		
The Flow	Chase Game	
Where is Nowhere?		

A second deck of cards is comprised of the game type cards. These are cards, each with the name of different instance-game types, together with a short explanation. A third deck of cards is optional, and comprised of the prop cards. These cards describe additional props the designer may want to use. Props may be artifacts associated with the performance (similar to theatrical props or costumes), or they can be *supporting technology*. The game-type and props card titles are listed in Table 1.

The cards are meant to be used on site, that is, where the future pervasive game is meant to be played. They can be used in a number of ways as part of the design process. Essentially the task for the designer is to design an instance-game concept on the basis of a combination of a mission card and a game type card (optionally narrowed by the use of a prop card), while making use of the actual physical site in question. For more details on the cards and the game see [5].

The design-game is meant to be played using a performative approach that adopts the special explorative mode of playfulness called *dérive*, which was devised by the *Situationist* movement [19]. This playful approach has also been found useful for participatory ethnographic fieldwork [29].

5.2   Accommodating the Situation: The Importance of Context

The design process affords the physical impact of the context. In the site-storming approach this component is created by physically locating the designer in the site where the instance-game (and thus the IS-artifact) will be operated. This process of in-situ design enables the designer to experience the constraints and affordances of the actual surroundings in which the software will operate. The design-games are centered on a ubiquitous game design that occurs in a specific (real-world) instance-game site. Consequently, the designer must be present in this physical site in order to best understand and accommodate the physical limits of the site, and to understand and take advantage of the physical affordances (in this case: the game affordances) available in the site.

5.3   Have Fun

The design process is fun because the design approach occurs within a game framework. The site-storming method incorporates this principle by devising the method as a playful activity in a game setting. This activity is accomplished by using mission-style game-setting and playing as a design approach, and the playful *dérive* attitude towards the design site. Mission-style games support creativity [2]. Such a fun, game-like design approach is more likely to yield a fun, game-like artifact because features of design approaches can infect the designed products. For example, systems development approaches that have been created using action research are often themselves characterized by features of action research in their orientation. Examples include Soft Systems Methodology [12] and Multiview [4].

5.4   Combine Individual and Group Work

The approach combines individual and group work by incorporating creative thinking individually and in groups by the means of competition in play. Play and games often combine individual tasks with group work. (For example, team games always rely on both the individual performer as well as the performance of the team as a whole). Using team-oriented approaches to creativity work relieves certain problems known to limit "Brainstorming" approaches [20], [23]. Examples of these problems include production blocking, social loafing, and fear of evaluation. Such unrestricted models of creativity (as in Brainstorming) can actually limit creativity, whereas minimal guidance and constraints, as in a creativity game, help the participants focus on the task in hand while minimizing the impact on creativity [15].

6   Evaluating the Specific Instance and the Method

Evaluation was complicated because we had to deal with two artifacts (the cliff game instance artifact and the design-game, which was itself an artifact of the approach). The surface relationship between the instance game artifact and the design-game artifact is not always clear. Although we may expect that a successful method should produce successful artifacts, it may be possible that a poor method may still produce successful artifacts and vice versa (this is due to the potential impact of individual creative talent). Because the performance of a creativity method (that is supposed to support and enhance the creativity of the designers) is subjective, it may be investigated using qualitative research. We chose to regard the method as successful if the designers approve of the method (the design-game), and there is evidence that the players enjoy the instance-game.

6.1   Evaluating the Specific Game

After the failed first attempt at designing the Cliff Game, the designers adopted the site-storming approach for designing the second prototype. By applying the site-storming method several aspects were redesigned. These concerned how the virtual part of the game fit with the site, how the players' locomotion affected the game and how the site supported the narrative. The soundscape of the Cliff Game was also redesigned to accommodate sonification to facilitate a better communication with the gamers. The redesigned version of the Cliff Game was play tested in a naturalistic ex post evaluation [56] during the summer of 2009. Three groups of two or three persons played the game. The test players were not the same persons who tested the first version, and as such did not have any previous knowledge of the game. After playing the game they were interviewed regarding their experience with the game. The results indicated that the redesign changed the game significantly. It was regarded as more fun and rewarding to locate the hotspots of the game using sonification than using a physical map. The players also sensed progression in the game more strongly as each hotspot was marked on the screen when found. Overall, the redesign using the site-storming method changed the experience of the Cliff Game from that of hearing an interactive narrative to that of playing a site-specific game.

6.2   Evaluating the Design Method

Evaluation of the method from the designers' point of view consisted of three series of evaluations with different designers, the first series as three design sessions in a partly artificial setting, the second series as a game design workshop in an artificial setting, and the third series as a design session in collaboration with a game developer working on a real problem. Summarizing on the four main creativity features, the evaluation of the site-storming method showed:

The design process provokes creativity. Evaluation of the method showed that the designers came up with several (typically 2-3) game concepts as a result of each session using the site-storming method. It also showed that the balance between the restrictions of a game and free creativity is important, and that designers may not agree upon these restrictions. Therefore the introduction of variations to prevent fatigue is important. The evaluation showed that the rule-bound nature of a game guides the users toward the task of creating ideas. Evaluation also supported that the method furthered divergent thinking, which is important when fostering new ideas (cf. [48]).

The design process affords an impact by the context. The concepts produced by working with the site-storming method were almost all directly connected to the context of the design sessions. The first series of evaluation showed that working on-site when developing new ideas for pervasive games furthers the creativity. All participant found that working in-situ radically had changed their way of thinking and that the result would have been different if they had worked in their usual context.

The design process is fun. The participants found the method fun and stimulating. They found working in-situ particularly inspiring.

The approach replicates the game idea and incorporates creative thinking individually and competitively. The game concept replicates the game idea by fulfilling the site-specific game model. Individual creative thinking was promoted by working individually while creating game concepts, but working collectively and in competitively when presenting them. The participants found it stimulating to be forced to work individually (they were used to work in teams) and then afterwards in groups when they developed the ideas. For full details of the evaluation see [34].

7   Site-Storming as an Explanatory Design Theory

Brooks [9] distinguishes design theory from instance theory by borrowing Plato's conceptualization of abstract thought from *The Republic* [42]: "Let us take any common instance; there are beds and tables in the world – plenty of them, are there not? *'Yes'*. But there are only two ideas or forms of them – one the idea of a bed, the other of a table." The idea of a chair is something on which we — humans — can sit removed from the coldness of the ground. The concrete instance of the chair can have one, two, three, four, five or more legs, but the abstract idea of the form of a chair remains the same.

We use this distinction in formulating explanatory design theory. The explanatory site-storming design theory (Figure 1) is the abstract idea or the meta-level [57] of a game. The concrete instance is "The Cliff Game". What is different from the example of the chair is that the abstract idea describes a process or a method for solving a certain kind of problem, namely site-specific game design. What is also different is that in describing such a process, we produce an artifact (in the form of a set of cards and their use). Thus part of the meta-level design theory is itself an artifact.

Another issue of importance is the balance between structure (in this case the rules and cards of the site-storming method) and creativity. Structure has a number of advantages. First, by following a structure, we facilitate the transfer of knowledge about better practices. Second, structure makes it easier to concentrate on one thing at a time in depth. Third, structure can include templates and examples that make it much easier to move forward. Fourth, new-comers to game design will learn more easily when aided by structure.

However, structure may also harm creativity by confining thinking, discouraging lateral thinking, and reducing the openness to experience [38]. On the other hand unfettered 'pure' creativity will inhibit knowledge transfer, concentration in-depth, and learning by new-comers. In the field of creativity games, where we wish the participants to produce new ideas, the lack of constraints is just as harmful as the presence of too many constraints (cf. [7], [8], [15]). Too many constraints in the form of complicated game rules shift the focus from idea generation to the instance-game itself, while too few constraints (an open game) may lead to fatigue and loss of interest in the design-game.

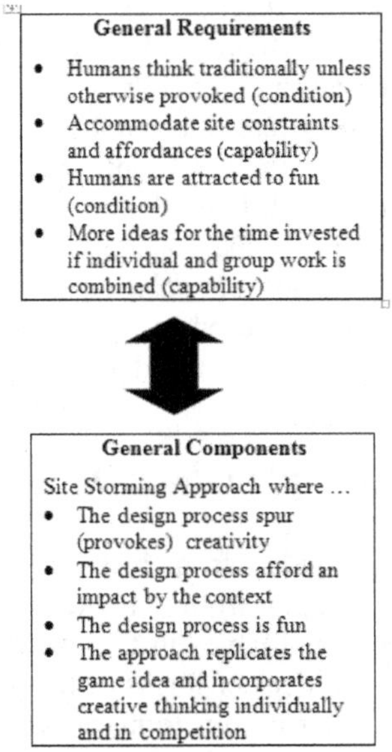

General Requirements

- Humans think traditionally unless otherwise provoked (condition)
- Accommodate site constraints and affordances (capability)
- Humans are attracted to fun (condition)
- More ideas for the time invested if individual and group work is combined (capability)

General Components

Site Storming Approach where ...
- The design process spur (provokes) creativity
- The design process afford an impact by the context
- The design process is fun
- The approach replicates the game idea and incorporates creative thinking individually and in competition

Fig. 1. An Explanatory Design Theory for site-storming design

These four general requirements, detailed also in section 5, are represented in the top box in Figure 1. This box represents the general requirements in an explanatory design theory [5]. The general components of the site-storming approach to design, i.e., the design-game components are represented in the bottom box in Figure 1.

8   Conclusion

We set out to explore if science and creativity could be combined in a design theory. By using a design science study described above, we developed an explanatory design theory [5] for site-storming game design. In doing so it combined – or "balanced" – the rigor of science research with fun. At the same time it provoked creativity, combining of individual and group work, and accommodating site specific constraints.

Besides building the design, evaluation is an important element in design science research. Given the subjectivity in appraising "fun", "creative", etc., we used qualitative techniques to capture the evaluation by users (game players) and designers. Approval by the people in the field was the main criterion for measuring the validity of the design theory and the usefulness of the artifacts. This naturalistic ex-post evaluation of the site-specific game method found approval by the designers, and the design theory successfully produced useful design artifacts when used by different designers.

We answer our research question on *"How can we balance creativity and science in information systems design settings?"* in the form of the explanatory design theory. By equating structure and science, we find that science and creativity can coexist theoretically in the form of a structured method that intends to provoke creativity by attending to the four general requirements of our game design theory. If carefully designed, it is possible to have ideal creativity and ideal structures (like method, logic, and analysis) operating in the same design process. However it has to be carefully balanced. Our work showed that if the design method is too structured in practice it hampers creativity, and if too unstructured it does not deliver game concepts of sufficient quality. Balancing creativity and structure is thus not always an easy task, and may not be possible under different circumstances, even when using the same design method. However our study shows one instance where science and creativity operated in a balanced way in the same design process.

When we design, there is almost always an element of the not-yet-known. By not-yet-known, we mean completely unknown because some un-designed artifact does not yet exist. We must accommodate creativity to discover the not-yet-known. But relying only on creativity increases the possibility of producing artifacts of varying quality. The science in design can improve the consistency (reliability) in artifact quality. But the science must balance structure and creativity in an ideal way without eliminating either.

References

1. Amabile, T.M.: How to kill creativity. Harvard Business Review 76(5), 76–87 (1998)
2. Anderson, K., McGonigal, J.: Place Storming: performing new technologies in context, NordiCHI 2004 Conference in Tampere, Finland. In: Proceedings of the Third Nordic Conference on Human-Computer Interaction, pp. 85–88. ACM, New York (2004)
3. Archer, L.B.: Systematic Method for Designers. The Design Council, London (1965)
4. Avison, D., Wood-Harper, A.: Multiview: An exploration in information systems development, pp. 54–59. McGraw Hill, London (1990)
5. Baskerville, R., Pries-Heje, J.: Explanatory Design Theory. Business & Information Systems Engineering 2(5), 271–282 (2010)
6. Bianco, A.T., Tory Higgins, E., Klem, A.: How "Fun/Importance" Fit Affects Performance: Relating Implicit Theories to Instruction. Personal and Social Psychological Bulletin 29(9), 1091–1103 (2003)
7. Brandt, E.: Designing Exploratory Design Games: A Framework for Participation in Participatory Design? In: Participatory Design Conference, Trento, Italy (August 2006)

8. Brandt, E., Messeter, J.: Facilitating collaboration through design games. In: Proceedings of the Eighth Conference on Participatory Design: Artful Integration: Interweaving Media, Materials and Practices, vol. 1, ACM, Toronto (2004)

9. Brooks, F.P.: The Design of Design: Essays from a Computer Scientist. Addison-Wesley, Upper Saddle River (2010)

10. Brown, T.: Change by design: How design thinking transforms organizations and inspires innovation. Harper Collins, New York (2009)

11. Caillois, R.: Man, Play, and Games (translated from French "Les Jeux et les hommes", 1958). University of Illinois Press, Urbana & Chicago (1961)

12. Checkland, P.: Systems Thinking, Systems Practice. J. Wiley, Chichester (1981)

13. Coverley, M.: Psychogeography, Harpenden, UK (2006)

14. Cross, N.: Forty years of design research. Design Studies 28(1), 1–4 (2007)

15. Dansey, N., Stevens, B.: Facilitating Creativity without Restrictions: A Pilot Implementation of an Idea Generation Game. In: MindTrek 2008 - The 12th International Conference on Entertainment and Media in the Ubiquitous Era, October 7-9. ACM, Tampere (2008)

16. De Bono, E.: New think; the use of lateral thinking in the generation of new ideas. Basic Books, New York (1968)

17. De Bono, E.: The mechanism of mind. Simon & Schuster, New York (1969)

18. De Bono, E.: Lateral thinking - creativity step by step. Harper & Row, New York (1970)

19. Debord, G.: Society of the Spectacle, New 1992 edn. Rebel Press, London (1992)

20. Diehl, M., Stroebe, W.: Productivity loss in idea-generating groups: tracking down the blocking effect. Journal of Personality and Social Psychology 61, 392–403 (1991)

21. Dorst, K.: Design Problems and Design Paradoxes. Design Issues 22(3), 4–17 (2006)

22. Fein, G.: Pretend play: creativity and consciousness. In: Gorlitz, P., Wohlwill, J. (eds.) Curiosity, Imagination, and Play. Lawrence Erlbaum Associates, Hillsdale (1987)

23. Furnham, A., Yazdanpanahi, T.: Personality Differences and Group versus Individual Brainstorming. Personality and Individual Differences 19(1), 73–80 (1995)

24. Guilford, J.P.: The Nature of Human Intelligence. McGraw Hill, New York (1967)

25. Guilford, J.P.: Transformative abilities or functions. Journal of Creative Behavior 17, 75–86 (1983)

26. Hatchuel, A.: Towards design theory and expandable rationality: the unfinished program of Herbert Simon. Journal of Management and Governance 5(3-4) (2002)

27. Iivari, J.: Distinguishing and contrasting two strategies for design science research. European Journal of Information Systems, 1–9 (2014)

28. Jansson, D., Smith, S.: Design fixation. Design Studies 12(1), 3–11 (1991)

29. Johansson, M., Linde, P.: Playful collaborative exploration: New research practice in participatory design. Journal of Research Practice 1(1), 1–18 (2005)

30. Kelley, T.: The ten faces of innovation Currency. Random House, Doubleday (2005)

31. Kelley, T., Littman, J.: The Art of Innovation: Lessons in Creativity from IDEO, America's Leading Design Firm. Broadway Business (2001)

32. Koen, P., Ajamian, G., Burkart, R., Clamen, A., Davidson, J., D'Amore, R., Elkins, C., Herald, K., Incorvia, M., Johnson, A., Karol, R., Seibert, R., Slavejkov, A., Wagner, K.: Providing clarity and a common language to the "fuzzy front end.". Research-Technology Management 44(2), 46–55 (2001)

33. Kristiansen, E.: Computer Games for the Real World. PhD-thesis, Roskilde University, Denmark (2010)

34. Kristiansen, E.: Design Games for In-Situ Design. International Journal of Mobile Human Computer Interaction (IJMHCI) 5(3), 1–22 (2013), doi:10.4018/jmhci.2013070101

35. Le Dantec, C.A.: Situated Design: Toward an Understanding of Design Through Social Creation and Cultural Cognition, C&C 2009, October 26–30. ACM, Berkeley (2009)
36. Le Masson, P., Hatchuel, A., Weil, B.: The Interplay between Creativity Issues and Design Theories: A New Perspective for Design Management Studies? Creativity and Innovation Management 20(4), 217–237 (2011)
37. MacCormack, A., Verganti, R., Iansiti, M.: Developing products on" Internet time": The anatomy of a flexible development process. Management Science 47(1), 133–150 (2001)
38. McCrae, R.R.: Creativity, divergent thinking, and openness to experience. Journal of Personality and Social Psychology 52(6), 1258–1265 (1987)
39. Montola, M., Stenros, J., Waern, A.: Pervasive Games – Theory and Design. Morgan Kaufman Publ, Amsterdam (2009)
40. Orlikowski, W.J., Iacono, C.S.: Research commentary: Desperately seeking "IT" in IT research - A call to theorizing the IT artifact. Information Systems Research 12(2), 121–134 (2001)
41. Oulasvirta, A., Kurvinen, E., Kankainen, T.: Understanding contexts by being there: case studies in bodystorming. Personal and Ubiquitous Computing 7(2), 125–134 (2003)
42. Plato: The Republic (360 BC)
43. Power, D.J.: Decision Support Systems. A historical overview. In: Power, D.J. (ed.) Handbook on Decision Support Systems, vol. 1. Springer (2008)
44. Purao, S., Baldwin, C., Hevner, A., Storey, V.C., Jan, P.-H., Smith, B., Zhu, Y.: The Sciences of Design: Observations on an Emerging Field. Communications of the Association for Information Systems (23), 1 (2008)
45. Purcell, A.T., Gero, J.S.: Design and other types of fixation. Design Studies 17(4), 363–383 (1996)
46. Reid, S.E., De Brentani, U.: The fuzzy front end of new product development for discontinuous innovations: a theoretical model. Journal of Product Innovation Management 21(3), 170–184 (2004)
47. Rittel, H., Webber, M.: Dilemmas in a General Theory of Planning. Policy Sciences (4), 155–169 (1973)
48. Runco, M.A.: Divergent Thinking, Ablex, Norwood, NJ, USA (1991)
49. Russ, S.W.: Affect and Creativity: the role of affect and play in the creative process. Lawrence Erlbaum Associates, Hillsdale (1993)
50. Russ, S.W.: Play and Creativty: developmental issues. Scandinavian Journal of Educational Research 47(3), 291–303 (2003)
51. Schechner, R.: Performance Studies: An Introduction. Routledge, London (2002)
52. Simon, H.A.: The Sciences of the Artificial, 3rd edn. MIT Press, Cambridge (1996)
53. Singer, J.L., Singer, D.L.: The House of Make-believe. Harvard University Press, Cambridge (1990)
54. Sosa, R., Gero, J.S.: Design and change: a model of situated creativity. In: Creative situations. IJCAI Creativity Workshop, University of Sydney (2003)
55. Sutton-Smith, B.: The Ambiguity of Play, 2001 paperback edn. First Harvard University Press, Cambridge (1997)
56. Venable, J., Pries-Heje, J., Baskerville, R.: A Comprehensive Framework for Evaluation in Design Science Research. In: Peffers, K., Rothenberger, M., Kuechler, B. (eds.) DESRIST 2012. LNCS, vol. 7286, pp. 423–438. Springer, Heidelberg (2012)
57. Walls, J.G., Widmeyer, G.R., El Sawy, O.A.: Building an information system design theory for vigilant EIS. Information Systems Research 3(1), 36–59 (1992)
58. Winter, R.: Design science research in Europe. European Journal of Information

Eight Types of Relationships between Stakeholders in ERP Development Networks: A Case Study of Three Large Enterprises

Andrey Maglyas and Kari Smolander

Software Engineering and Information Management
Lappeenranta University of Technology, Finland
{andrey.maglyas,kari.smolander}@lut.fi

Abstract. ERP projects are complex socio-technical endeavors that cannot be implemented and used in isolation. Instead, many stakeholders are involved in the implementation of ERP systems. However, the ERP research often concentrates on relationships between two stakeholders only. In this study we take a broader viewpoint to relationships between external stakeholders in ERP development networks. We investigated the ERP development networks of three global enterprises and revealed eight types of relationships between the stakeholders. Understanding of what types of relationships exist is important for locating potential problems. As an example, we describe how an overtrusted relationship can lead to technical challenges.

Keywords: ERP development network, case study, stakeholders, relationships.

1 Introduction

The adoption and use of ERP systems involve many stakeholders but ERP research often concentrates on the viewpoint of one stakeholder only [1]. Being a complex information system, an ERP system requires support from many levels and organizations including the flagship organization (e.g. SAP, Microsoft, Oracle) [2], consultants, 3rd party development organizations, and IT support and administration. All these and other stakeholders altogether form an ERP network of stakeholders with dissimilar culture, practices, and processes but united by the same goal of implementing and deploying an ERP system.

It has been identified that ERP projects often have key players and without these players an ERP project is prone to failure [3]. However, the ERP research community is lacking evidence about ERP development networks, their challenges, and interactions and mainly concentrates on ERP failures [4] and success factors [5] from the perspective of the system user only. The research on human interactions in systems development also focuses primary on single organizations and their internal communications [6].

Being an example of a socio-technical endeavor that involve both social interactions between stakeholders and technical aspects of implementation and

T.H. Commisso et al. (Eds.): SCIS 2014, LNBIP 186, pp. 58–73, 2014.
© Springer International Publishing Switzerland 2014

integration [7], ERP systems require deeper understanding of the complex process of ERP development, its participants, and relationships between them. In this paper, we focus on the latter part by making an inquiry into ERP development in three global enterprises. We analyze three ERP development networks (EDNs) in order to identify the types of relationships between stakeholders. The selected enterprises use both customized ERP systems from flagship organizations and fully customized ERP systems developed from scratch. This allowed us to investigate different kinds of ERP networks. They had variation in their groups of stakeholders, where e.g. the flagship organization or the development partner was emphasized differently.

The paper is organized as follows: we introduce the related work in Section 2. The research process and case study design are described in Section 3. The main findings are presented in Section 4, followed by the discussion of the results in Section 5. Section 6 concludes the paper.

2   Related Work

The term ERP development network is not commonly used in ERP research. However, there are similar terms like ERP community introduced by Sammon and Adam and defined as a group consisting of ERP vendors, consultants, and implementing organizations [8] or ERP ecosystem defined as the network created by collaborative partnerships between and among organizations [9]. Koch uses both terms ERP network and ERP community but mainly focuses on ERP vendors [10]. In general, an ERP development network (EDN) can be understood as a dynamic group of stakeholders from different levels and organizations involved into the lifecycle of an ERP system. The network includes ERP vendors that provide expertise and tools [4], consultants participating in the adoption of the system [11], 3rd party developers [12], and others.

As any network, EDN consists of nodes (stakeholders) and edges (relationships between stakeholders). Gefen studied the ERP implementation relationships between clients and vendors and identified that trust is an important component for building strong business relationships between the vendor and the client [13]. Sammon and Adam state that the implementing organization, the ERP vendor and the ERP consultant are the most important stakeholders and their relationships are critical for the success of ERP [8]. In contrast, Sarker revealed that other stakeholders like 3rd party organizations, hardware providers, and local partners also contribute to the ERP success [14].

Outsourcing has been widely used and studied from different perspectives in the development of ERP systems [15]. For example, Nam et al. investigated two levels of IS outsourcing: the initial outsourcing decision and the intention to continue the relationships [16]. They named four types of outsourcing relationships as reliance, alliance, support, and alignment based on the level of strategic impact of IS applications and the extent of substitution by vendors. Additionally, the authors concluded that continued relationships are possible only when vendors are not only technically competent but also trustworthy [16].

Overall, EDNs are nearly always global and consist of many stakeholders, but existing literature often concentrates only on relationships between two stakeholders, especially between the vendor and the customer [17] or between the customer and consultants [11]. As a result, the existing literature lacks identification and classification of stakeholders and their relationships in EDNs.

3   Case Study Design

Case study as a research method has been widely used in social sciences for a long time [18, 19]. In the field of information systems (IS) it also has a long history and it has been analyzed from many philosophical perspectives like positivism [20] and interpretivism [21]. Runeson and Höst [22] discuss that in the field of software engineering objects are different from what is studied in social sciences and information systems research. Software engineering researchers focus on organizations developing software rather than on organizations using software systems [22]. In this study, we focus on ERP development networks that include both developers and users of information systems as well as other supporting organizations like hardware and software vendors, consulting firms, and auditors. In this regard, the choice of the case study method is not occasional, because it has been previously used for studies in both software engineering and information systems fields. We selected a flexible exploratory case study design [18] in order to get a deep understanding of the studied phenomenon and used semi-structured interviews for data collection.

This study is a part of a large research project conducted by three universities with ten researchers involved. Six of them conducted interviews mostly in pairs. This generated large amount of qualitative data and in order to manage it, we followed the case study process consisting of five steps [19]: (1) Designing a case study; (2) Preparing for data collection (conducting a case study: phase 1); (3) Collecting the evidence (conducting a case study: phase 2); (4) Analyzing case study evidence; (5) Reporting.

The goal of this study was to identify the types of relationships between the stakeholders in ERP development networks and get an understanding of the impact of these relationships.

3.1   Designing a Case Study

The initial phase of the study aimed at defining the research questions to be studied. The idea for a case study was born during a brainstorming session that was held four months after the project started. The central topic of the brainstorming session was the identification of networks of stakeholders involved in ERP development in the cases. However, this discussion mainly focused on stakeholders. The present authors noted that a network consists of not only nodes but also relationships between these nodes. It was agreed that a study on relationships between stakeholders is required and the present authors took the responsibility to conduct this study. The initial research question was formulated as follows:

What types of relationships exist between stakeholders in ERP development networks?

Our case study is inductive by nature. We did not have any a priori framework for the study. In this regard, our approach is similar as that of the grounded theory research method [23], which is executed without a priori theories. Our research objective is exploratory and therefore we expected that the types of relationships will emerge as we start collecting and analyzing evidence.

3.2   Preparing for Data Collection

In this phase, the detailed procedures for conducting interviews were designed and preparations like contacting key persons in organizations were made. The interviews were designed to investigate the phenomenon of EDN in general rather than going into details of particular parties involved in EDN. The main purpose of the interviews was to identify the network itself and classify the relationships between stakeholders.

The interview guide was initially developed based on the research project goals. Every researcher contributed to the guide by adding new and revising existing questions to better fit the project goals. Then, the guide was reviewed and refined by other researchers several times. The final set of questions included open ended questions that allowed researchers to investigate particularly important details of EDNs without forcing the interviewees to a predefined interview structure.

When the guide was ready, we distributed an invitation letter to our key contacts in three case organizations. These organizations were our industry partners that represent large enterprises using and adopting ERP systems.

Case A is a large global manufacturing enterprise with an annual turnover over 9 billion euros. Case A decided to build a fully-customized ERP system for sales and logistics in order to replace several legacy systems and also to overcome the year 2000 problem without having to make the necessary updates to all the systems. The ERP system implementation started in the middle of 1990s because the existing system could not satisfy the enterprise requirements for supporting business processes of the domain and for controlling the complex supply chain. During the development that is still on going, the system went through major challenges like a redesign of the system architecture but the system is still in use globally. The network of stakeholders has been growing all the time. For example, nowadays the system is still in charge of supply chain processes but financial controlling and human resources are managed by a SAP ERP instance.

Case B is a global service provider in retail business. Case B has a close partnership with a small ERP vendor. Case B decided to start a renewal project because the old ERP system could not meet the requirements for supporting critical business processes. The project was initiated in 2008 but started really in 2010. Currently the system is under development and planned to support almost all business processes of the company including sales, inventory management, and customer relationship management. A software company is developing the ERP system for Case B exclusively, but the developer has plans to develop a packaged software product from the result.

Case C is a global manufacturing enterprise with over 20,000 employees. Case C has decided to implement a customized ERP system for raw material procurement together with an implementation partner. The project started in 2003 and the first version of the system was available in 2008. Five years later, the system still requires large investments in its development and maintenance.

The characteristics of the case organizations are briefly summarized in Table 1. Case A and Case C are similar because they both are large manufacturing enterprises with comparable number of employees. However, the approach to the adoption of ERP systems is different. Case A develops its own ERP system while Case C customizes an existing ERP package. Case B is more specific as it is a global service provider with different kind of business processes. The selection of these cases was mainly dictated by available research partners, but they represent a range of different ERP development networks.

Overall, our aim was to understand the types of relationships between stakeholders involved in an ERP project. For this reason, the cases were selected to represent a variation of organizations, ERP systems, and development projects.

Table 1. Overview of the organizations covered by this case study

Organization	Case A	Case B	Case C
Type of organization	Large global manufacturing enterprise	Global service provider in retail business	Global manufacturing enterprise
# of employees	29.000	1.500	20.000
Type of ERP system	Fully-customized ERP system developed from scratch	ERP system developed from scratch	Customized ERP system
Business areas covered by the ERP system	Sales and logistics	Sales, inventory management, CRM (~90% of all business processes)	Raw material procurement

3.3   Collecting the Evidence

A semi-structured interview strategy [18] with the snowballing technique [24] was used for the interviews. The interviews were conducted in a period of four months from February, 2013 to May, 2013. The interviews started from our key contacts in each of the three organizations and then next interviewees were referrals from previous ones. We were able to investigate the development network of the ERP project by navigating from one stakeholder to another. Overall, we concentrated on the experiences and asked questions about challenges, stakeholders, and reflections on the results of ERP projects. The questions were tailored for each interview as advised by Charmaz [24]. These variations were based on the role of the interviewee and his or her responsibilities, e.g. if an interviewee was a developer, we concentrated on technical questions and skipped the questions related to strategy. Therefore, the questions were mainly about the activities the interviewee was involved in but we also asked about the connections of the interviewee with other persons involved in the project and their roles and responsibilities. In addition, we asked questions about the subjective feelings of the project in order to understand the projects' overall perception. Table 2 presents the list of interviewees and their roles.

The interviews were conducted, recorded, and transcribed. The transcription process was done by a professional agency that put as much information as possible to the transcript including all hesitancies, pauses, and changes in intonation by taking necessary notes inside the transcripts. External events like phone calls interrupting the interviews were also documented. Overall, the interviews lasted from 30 to 111 minutes, with the average of about an hour.

Table 2. The roles of interviewees

Interview #	Case	Role
A1	A	IT manager of business area
A2	A	Program manager
A3	A	IT department representative of sales
A4	A	Project manager
A5	A	Vendor service owner
A6	A	Service manager
A7	A	Software manager
A8	A	Senior customer manager
A9	A	Continuous service manager
B1	B	Software specialist
B2	B	Lead designer
B3	B	Head of product development
B4	B	CEO
C1	C	IT service owner
C2	C	Architect
C3	C	Solution owner
C4	C	Global owner

3.4   Analyzing Case Study Evidence

The analysis of the collected and transcribed data was performed using a special tool for qualitative data analysis, Atlas.ti. In total, we collected more than 250 pages of qualitative data and to analyze the data we performed a three-step process consisting of coding, grouping, and interpretation.

Coding of the transcripts was similar to open coding in Grounded Theory [25]. The collected data were broken down analytically in order to understand what the pieces of data really mean. These pieces from different interviews were compared with each other to find differences and similarities and to give a conceptual label to each event/action/phenomenon. Then, the pieces of data with their labels were grouped together to form categories with subcategories, which represented a higher level of abstraction than the original data. Interpretation of the collected evidence consisted of identifying and elaborating of the categories relevant to research questions.

4   Results

By analyzing the data we identified ERP development stakeholders and their relationships in the three case organizations. In this section we concentrate only on the external relationships between organizations in ERP development networks. In addition, all these organizations have an internal network of stakeholders involved in their ERP projects. We however do not describe these here due to space limitations.

4.1   Case A

The external stakeholders for Case A are presented in Fig. 1. Case A has adopted a fully-customized ERP system developed from scratch and therefore the most important relationship in this EDN is between Case A and the development organization. We named this relationship cooperation but in reality this relationship was even stronger:

"Well, in general we have developed a so-called old marriage relationship with [Case A]. We are very familiar with one another, and that has been good. Sometimes it may even be a bit of a burden to know one another so well, but tight cooperation is good when working on challenging system development. Our people know Case A's IT people, and they know us, so the cooperation is painless. Challenges always arise, though, and there is always an effort to cut costs, but that's the norm today – A8.

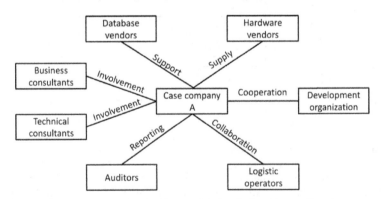

Fig. 1. External stakeholders and their relationships to Case A

In general, the cooperation between Case A and development organization was considered to be positive but it was not painless. The project duration and budget was exceeded but at that time Case A could not any more change the developer:

"Even though it was a fixed-price project, our management gave in to [Development organization] because this caused them such big losses so we paid some more

after all. Exceeding the original budget and time frame significantly could've also been the end of the project but the management had faith in the project and us." – A1.

In addition, Case A trusted the development organization, which was identified as the main reason for upcoming technical problems:

"...technology is the only thing that we should've, we were a little too trusting when [Development organization] said that their two-level architecture would work with high enough performance. Of course we had performance guarantee in the agreement and everything but... we were too trusting and so were [Development organization] so we should've look far deeper into that and whether the technical specifications were adequate. So in that we were a little amateurish. I guess [Case A] we trusted too much that [Development organization] knows what it's doing but they didn't. They just counted on the same grounds as before but didn't confirm the functioning. So this was maybe the most amateurish mistake" – A1.

In order to overcome the technical and performance problems, Case A decided to hire additional technical consultants and involved them in the development of the ERP system. The consultants played an important role in changing the ERP architecture from two-tier to three-tier, which is the solution used today. Although they made changes in the architecture, the relationship was not as close as with the development organization. We consider this connection weaker than cooperation and call it involvement. There was a very similar situation with external business consultants that took part in the planning phase of the system due to the complexity of business processes. The business consultants were involved in the project and actively participated in the development and tailoring of business processes within the case organization.

Initially, a database vendor provided a solution for the ERP system and supported its database. However, the costs went up and the database vendor was not willing to be flexible and supportive. The situation ended up in conflict and Case A decided to switch to another database vendor:

"...they were very willing to tune the service according to our needs and license-wise they were also cheaper. And things ran smoothly with [Database vendor] for a couple of years but then... they weren't as flexible anymore so we decided to, and the technology developed so that [Database vendor 2] evolved to be an attractive and affordable solution also for this kind of systems... " – A2.

Hardware vendors often provide solutions and hardware with limited potential for customization like adding more memory or installing a hard drive with more capacity. In contrast with hardware vendors, database vendors have more opportunities for creating highly customized solution for a particular organization. It can include database tuning for a specific data set used in the organization or optimizing database performance. Therefore, we distinguish between these two types of relationships as support and supply. It reflects the difference between delivering the solution only and supporting own solution with customer specific help in the adoption.

External auditors were hired during the ERP project to do an analysis of different ERPs and advise what the best option is. As our interviewees remember this situation, the relationships between Case A and the auditors were formal and the auditors' main role was in performing an analysis and reporting to the top management. It was the most formal relationship we observed in Case A.

"At that point, I think [External auditor] was the company that performed the analysis and concluded that [the developed ERP system] is the best option to use. Various benchmarks have also been done to other ERP systems, such as what differences exist between the ERP products. Since we have a customized ERP, the customer once wanted to know about the differences between SAP and [our system], so there we of course used SAP consultants, both internal and external" – A5.

Case A also closely collaborates with logistics operators. The ERP system has connections to various logistics providers and it is partially integrated with their systems. This relationship is important for the business of both parties but their information systems operate independently.

"I suppose you could consider them stakeholders in a way. But they are not giving us any sort of definitions; the system simply has connections to these third parties." – A6.

Overall, the relationships in EDN of Case A vary from very formal as with external auditors to very informal and cooperative so-called "forced marriage" as with the development organization. Trust to the development organization led to the technical issues that could not be overcome internally and therefore external technical consultants and auditors were needed to change the system architecture and evaluate other possible ERP systems for the adoption.

4.2   Case B

The external stakeholders for Case B are presented in Fig. 2. Case B also adopts an ERP system developed from scratch but its EDN is simpler than in Case A. Case B was a part of the supplier in the past, but then it was separated as a global service provider. Still, it collaborates with the main company and this relationship is strong in terms of business cooperation.

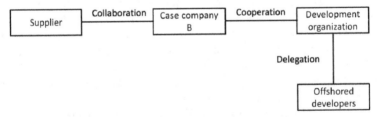

Fig. 2. External stakeholders and their relationships to Case B

The relationship between Case B and the development organization seems to be very common in terms of roles: Case B provides feature requests and bug reports, the development organization makes their prioritization and bug fixes.

"It's a system in production and everybody understands what it means for the office. We haven't had problems with that. Mostly the problem has been, or the challenge has been to agree the most important things with [Case B], so that it doesn't spread too much, because we can't do everything. Before we have the internal

prioritization and tracking meetings, that we know what the customer wants and what is most urgent, we occasionally specify them." – B2.

Case B has been working with the development organization for a long time.

"*I think the cooperation has been good all the time. Of course the history of [Cas B's] and [the development organization]'s cooperation as partners is so long, so we have earned the trust which also helps in this situation. But I have been involved with [Case B] people even before the actual deployment project, so I know them as stakeholders and as a customer. So the cooperation is straightforward in that way.*" – B3.

However, trust cannot be really observed from the interviews. In contrast, we observed very formal processes like documenting all feature requests, regular steering group meetings, and the use of project management and bug tracking tools.

The development organization has used offshoring development tasks widely. We named this relationship delegation. The delegation of the development tasks was mainly done for cost-cutting reasons. However, it had no significant effects to the quality of the final product because the development organization has dedicated persons for testing the offshored code and they perform the final approval of the code.

Overall, Case B reminds conventional development of a software product rather than the development of an ERP system. The development organization has plans to sell the developed ERP system as a product to other customers later. The relationship between Case B and the development organization is based on trust but still quite formal. Currently the ERP system is in the piloting phase waiting for rollouts.

4.3   Case C

The external stakeholders for Case C are presented in Fig. 3. Case C is also adopting a customized ERP system. The main parts of this system were acquired from a vendor, but support was still required to tailor the system to the needs of the business at Case C.

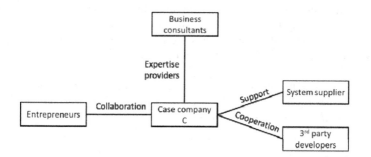

Fig. 3. External stakeholders and their relationships to Case C

The relationship between Case C and the system supplier was identified as support because the system supplier not only provides the ERP system, but also constantly supports the case company by implementing new components to the system. In addition, in this case 3rd party developers play an important role in developing additional components to the ERP system. This relationship is similar to the relationships between the case company and the development organization in the other two cases:

"[System supplier] is our main system supplier. There are also different kinds of support services. [3rd party developer] provides us with the feedback service through which we transfer messages from [The ERP system] to [Another system] and [Yet another system], these mobile devices, and so on. The application side deals with [System supplier] to a large extent. Other companies do some things like further development for these applications, let's say they support services." – C2.

The case company actively collaborates with individual entrepreneurs and small companies that provide raw materials to the company. The case company calls them entrepreneurs. Beyond participation in the business, they also provide input and feature requests to the ERP system.

"Well yeah, of course our entrepreneurs... our operations are based on entrepreneurs... being outside parties who do all this work, so at least these entrepreneurs participated at some point. We were also making different kinds of parts of the system for entrepreneurs, parts that they are now using." – C3.

Due to the complexity of the business processes, external expertise was required for customizing the ERP system to daily use. It was done through recruiting external consultants, who had expertise in developing and customizing ERP systems in complex environments. Consultants did not participate directly to the implementation, but acted only as a source of expertise.

"We kind of bought this kind of project methodology as a ready package, so we didn't need to design that from the beginning. We pretty much used the ready package we bought. And of course at some point when the project had matured enough and we were finished with the specifications, that's when we had the actual bidding competition and the winner of that competition of course began doing more specifications with us" – C3.

Case C adopts a customized ERP system and therefore its EDN is simple in terms of the number of external stakeholders involved. Only the vendor, several 3rd party developers and external consultants were involved in the project. They all took part in customizing the ERP system to the needs of Case C. However, the relationships between Case C and external stakeholders were not very trusted. The system provider also provided services to the competitors and the case company tried to minimize the lack of expertise outside the company.

"As long as [System provider] also provides services to our competitors, if they learn through this project new perspectives or new ways of doing things, of course they can exploit that even with our competitors." – C4.

4.4   Summary

In Table 3 we summarize the identified types of relationships between the case organizations and external stakeholders involved in the development of ERP systems. In total, we identified eight types of relationships: cooperation, collaboration, reporting, involvement, expertise providers, support, supply, and delegation but only two types (cooperation and collaboration) were common for all cases. Other relationships like reporting and supply were identified in one case only but they do not seem to be unique. Whether these relationships are present in an EDN depends on the activities like hiring auditors and purchasing hardware.

Table 3. Types of relationships between the case companies and external stakeholders

Types of relationships	Description	Cases	Stakeholders
Cooperation	Both parties act together for the mutual benefit. The relationship is characterized by a relatively high level of openness from both sides.	Case A, Case B, Case C	(The case company)-(The development organization); (The case company)-(3rd party developers)
Collaboration	Both parties work for selfish benefit but act together for the synergy benefit. The level of openness is low.	Case A, Case B, Case C	(The case company)-(Logistic operators); (The case company)-(Supplier); (The case company)-(Entrepreneurs)
Reporting	One party evaluates the situation and reports the results.	Case A	(The case company)-(Auditors)
Involvement	One party is not only evaluates the situation but also introduces and implements changes (business or technical) in the organization.	Case A	(The case company)-(Technical consultants); (The case company)-(Business consultants)
Expertise providers	The organization buys knowledge and expertise but introduces and/or implements it internally itself.	Case C	(The case company)-(Business consultants)
Support	The solution (database, system, and etc.) is not only provided and delivered but also is customized for the needs of particular organization.	Case A, Case C	(The case company)-(Database vendor); (The case company)-(System supplier)
Supply	The solution (e.g. servers) is only delivered but additional customizations are predefined and very limited.	Case A	(The case company)-(Hardware vendor)
Delegation	A part of development is outsourced to another stakeholder with the following control of the quality of the results.	Case B	(The case company)-(Offshored developers)

5   Discussion

5.1   Types of Relationships

By investigating three large enterprises we identified eight types of relationships between ERP user organizations and external stakeholders. Both Case A and Case B adopted ERP systems developed from scratch. Therefore, they both actively work with a development organization. We called this relationship cooperation. Gefen considered trust as an important component for building strong relationships [13]. However, in Case A we observed that the case company overtrusted the decisions made by the development organization. It led to technical problems that could not be easily overcome. In this regard, our results contradict to some extent with the Gefen's observations. Although some level of trust between stakeholders is needed as we observed in Case B, the trust should not prevent critical evaluation of the technical and business decisions made by external stakeholders.

Case C adopts an ERP system, the main components of which were bought from the vendor. Then, both the vendor and the 3rd party developers provided support and developed new components for the customer. This was previously considered as a possible way to success in ERP projects [17] and our case contributes to this body of knowledge by providing one more case. However, in our case the support relationship was also observed between the customer and the database vendor. The role of the database vendor in case of developing an ERP system from scratch is not limited to providing the solution (the supply relationship) but also to tuning the database to the organization's needs. In this regard, the database vendor can be added as another stakeholder that contributes to the success of ERP system in addition to the ERP vendor and the ERP consultants as described in [8].

In case A there was a clear division between technical and business consultants that we did not observe in other cases. However, both technical and business consultants were involved in the ERP project to resolve technical and business challenges [11]. In case of business consultants we have observed two types of relationships: involvement and expertise providers. Involvement means that the consultants were involved in the development activities and actively participated in the ERP project. In contrast, the role of expertise providers was in bringing the expertise about business processes but they had no role in or direct impact on the development activities. In addition to consultants, auditors participated in one of the three ERP projects as independent evaluators of a different ERP system. Auditors are not commonly used in ERP projects and therefore they are rarely considered as part of an EDN [9, 10].

In addition to cooperation between the customer and the development organization, we found another weaker type of this relationship that we called collaboration. This relationship was observed in all cases between the case companies and logistic operators (Case A), supplier (Case B), or entrepreneurs (Case C). In all cases they could ask for additional feature requests that were transferred by the case company to development organization or system supplier. In this regard, the case company was a link in the network to transfer knowledge from one part of the network to another [26]. The relationship cooperation corresponds to the reliance relationship in terms of [16]. This is the most common type of relationship in outsourcing with cost reduction as the major motivation.

An ERP project requires contribution from many development organizations [12] and therefore 3rd party developers are often involved. In Case A the development organizations delegated some development functions to other companies. Although it was done for cost-saving reasons, it can lead to unpredictable life cycle costs and risks related to the availability of offshore developers for a long time [27]. In Case C the case company itself worked with 3rd party developers in order to implement some additional features. Hiring 3rd party develop was identified as a reasonable approach when extensive customization and programming of enterprise systems are needed [28]. In this case, the 3rd party developer also supported the case company with the provided solution.

5.2 Implications and Limitations

With this study we make the first step toward creating a theory of relationships in ERP development networks. According to Gregor's taxonomy, the theory relates to the explanation type of theories [29]. Rather than making predictions on the impact of relationships to the ERP system success, we explain that different types of relationships and their combinations are possible.

With the three cases studied, the scope of validity of the theory is limited [28]. However, it creates a basis for forming the theory scope of interest and extending the scope of validity to the scope of interest with new studies.

We consider the presented results as a Level 1 theory in which only minor working relationships between constructs that are based on direct observations are established [30]. Therefore, the results should be iteratively refined and developed based on new cases to progress the theory to levels 2 and 3.

The study has also limitations. The use of snowballing technique [23] for navigating through the EDNs aimed to cover the network as much as possible. However, it was the first round of interviews and some parts of the networks have not been investigated so far. As it can be observed from Table 2, the number of interviews is not balanced well and we studied Case A in more detail. More interviews in Case B and C could reveal new types of relationships but we did not manage to identify other external stakeholders using the snowballing technique. Another risk is related to confidentiality issues. Although we guaranteed anonymity for both interviewees' names and company names, our research topic and questions were quite sensitive and therefore some information could be hidden from us.

6 Conclusion

Successful and efficient implementation and adoption of ERP systems require contribution from and involvement of many stakeholders. However, the ERP endeavors are often studied from the viewpoint of relationships between two stakeholders only [1, 6, 11]. In this study we took a broader look at ERP development networks at three large enterprises and identified eight types of relationships between external stakeholders. Instead of going into details of relationships, we provided a general overview of the types of relationships observed in real life. ERP projects rarely go smoothly [4] and the problems can occur from the lack of understanding of relationships between stakeholders. For example, in this study we observed that the overtrusted relationship between the customer and the development organization can lead to serious technical problems in the project.

In summary, our study reports on the existing types of relationships between the ERP user and its external stakeholders in three global enterprises. The identified types of relationships aim at increasing our understanding of ERP systems as complex and dynamic endeavors where challenges can come from any stakeholder.

Acknowledgements. This study was supported by Academy of Finland grant #259454.

References

1. Skok, W., Legge, M.: Evaluating enterprise resource planning (ERP) systems using an interpretive approach. Knowledge and Process Management 9, 72–82 (2002)
2. Ernst, D., Kim, L.: Global production networks, knowledge diffusion, and local capability formation. Research Policy 31, 1417–1429 (2002)
3. Somers, T.M., Nelson, K.G.: A taxonomy of players and activities across the ERP project life cycle. Information & Management 41, 257–278 (2004)
4. Xue, Y., Liang, H., Boulton, W.R., Snyder, C.A.: ERP implementation failures in China: Case studies with implications for ERP vendors. International Journal of Production Economics 97, 279–295 (2005)
5. Al-Mashari, M., Al-Mudimigh, A., Zairi, M.: Enterprise resource planning: A taxonomy of critical factors. European Journal of Operational Research 146, 352–364 (2003)
6. Hannakaisa Isomäki, S.P.: Reframing Humans in Information Systems Development. Springer 201, 1–14 (2010)
7. Porto De Albuquerque, J., Simon, E.J.: Dealing with Socio-Technical Complexity: Towards a Transdisciplinary Approach to IS Research. In: European Conference on Information Systems ECIS, pp. 1458–1468 (2007)
8. Sammon, D., Adam, F.: Decision Making in the ERP Community. In: ECIS 2002 Proceedings (2002)
9. Antero, M., Riis, P.H.: Strategic Management of Network Resources: A Case Study of an ERP Ecosystem. International Journal of Enterprise Information Systems 7, 18–33 (2011)
10. Koch, C.: ERP a Moving Target. International Journal of Business Information Systems 2, 426–443 (2007)
11. Metrejean, E., Stocks, M.H.: The Role of Consultants in the Implementation of Enterprise Resource Planning Systems. Academy of Information and Management Sciences Journal 14, 1–25 (2011)
12. Brehm, L., Heinzl, A., Markus, M.L.: Tailoring ERP systems: a spectrum of choices and their implications. In: Proceedings of the 34th Annual Hawaii International Conference on System Sciences, pp. 9–18 (2001)
13. Gefen, D.: What Makes an ERP Implementation Relationship Worthwhile: Linking Trust Mechanisms and ERP Usefulness. Journal of Management Information Systems 21, 263–288 (2004)
14. Suprateek Sarker, A.S.L.: Using a case study to test the role of three key social enablers in ERP implementation. Information & Management, 813–829 (2003)
15. Information Systems Outsourcing - Enduring Themes, New Perspectives and Global Challenges
16. Nam, K., Rajagopalan, S., Rao, H.R., Chaudhury, A.: A Two-level Investigation of Information Systems Outsourcing. Communications of ACM 39, 36–44 (1996)

17. Addo-Tenkorang, R., Helo, P.: Enterprise Resource Planning (ERP): A Review Literature Report. In: Proceedings of the World Congress on Engineering and Computer Science 2011, WCECS, vol. II (2011)
18. Robson, C.: Real world research: a resource for users of social research methods in applied settings. Wiley, Chichester (2011)
19. Yin, R.: Case study research: design and methods. Sage Publications (2002)
20. Lee, A.S.: A scientific methodology for MIS case studies. MIS Quarterly 13, 33 (1989)
21. Klein, H.K., Myers, M.D.: A set of principles for conducting and evaluating interpretive field studies in information systems. MIS Quarterly 23, 67–93 (1999)
22. Runeson, P., Höst, M.: Guidelines for conducting and reporting case study research in software engineering. Empirical Software Engineering 14, 131–164 (2009)
23. Strauss, A., Corbin, J.: Basics of Qualitative Research: Techniques and Procedures for Developing Grounded Theory. SAGE Publications (2008)
24. Charmaz, K.: Constructing grounded theory. Sage Publications, London (2006)
25. Corbin, J., Strauss, A.: Grounded Theory Research: Procedures, Canons, and Evaluative Criteria. Qualitative Sociology 13, 3–21 (1990)
26. Simonin, B.L.: Ambiguity and the process of knowledge transfer in strategic alliances. Strategic Management Journal 20, 595–623 (1999)
27. Olson, D.L.: Evaluation of ERP outsourcing. Computers & Operations Research 34, 3715–3724 (2007)
28. Jacobs, D.: Enterprise Software As Service. Queue 3, 36–42 (2005)
29. Gregor, S.: The Nature of Theory in Information Systems. MIS Quarterly 30, 611–642 (2006)
30. Sjøberg, D.I.K., Dybå, T., Anda, B.C.D., Hannay, J.E.: Building Theories in Software Engineering. In: Shull, F., Singer, J., Sjøberg, D.I.K. (eds.) Guide to Advanced Empirical Software Engineering, pp. 312–336. Springer, London (2008)

Designing Virtual Collaboration Environment for Distance Learners: Exploring Socialization as a Basis for Collaboration

Judith Molka-Danielsen and Ole David Brask

Molde University College, Molde, Norway
{J.Molka-Danielsen,Ole.D.Brask}@himolde.no

Abstract. This study investigates perceptions of university college students towards a virtual collaboration environment and explores the concept of support for socialization as a necessary basis for a collaborative writing task. The paper describes distant students' experiences of communicating and collaborating in a virtual world. The conceptual analysis is comprised of the theoretical perspectives of socio-constructivist learning and group processes are analyzed according to Time-Interaction-Performance (TIP) theory. Descriptive content analysis was used to analyze focus group data from 16 university college students, and the results were verified with participants. The findings show that although writing in the virtual world was hindered, students described in-world experiences of presence, awareness and belonging – considered to be important for the building of trust, negotiation of meaning and in fulfilling the collaborative task. Our results provide valuable implications for ways to increase well-being, member support and production in online collaborations.

Keywords: Computer-mediated communication, collaborative learning, distance education, Time-Interaction-Performance, virtual world environments.

1 Introduction

In increasingly mobile societies, distance learning is of growing importance within the social constructivist perspective of learning as stated by Vygotsky that learning is a social phenomenon, and that knowledge is a product of social interaction [1]. Online collaboration is a crucial part of the social element of learning and is a growing area of research [2]. The theoretical perspective of the socio-constructivist learning perspective constitutes a conceptual platform in this research.

Collaboration, in the social-constructivist perspective, is a natural and central part of education and prior research has examined the perspective of people engaged in collective learning in a shared domain where learning becomes a collaborative process of a group [3]. Prior research by Bjorn et al [4] examines capabilities and functions of groupware and looks at how "groupware adoption can be conceptualized as a three-step process of expanding and aligning individual technological frames towards groupware." [4, p.28] The three step process consists of comprising activities that bring knowledge of new technological opportunities to the participants, facilitating the participants to articulate and evaluate their work practices and their use

T.H. Commisso et al. (Eds.): SCIS 2014, LNBIP 186, pp. 74–89, 2014.
© Springer International Publishing Switzerland 2014

of technology and participants' committing to, and practical enactment of, groupware technology [4].

Our research similarly examines how collaborative technologies are used by groups. This research adopts a case study approach and to examine collaboration in a shared task of collaborative writing (CW). Further our research aims to aid designers of learning modules for geographically dispersed learners with the application of virtual world (VW) technologies and other communication technologies as a basis for the collaborative task. Through collaboration and negotiations people acquire a common understanding of shared knowledge. We recognize that CW is only one example of a shared knowledge space, where students come together as communities of learners to share knowledge as they generate content [5].

The case participants are distance learners in a Social Educators bachelors program in Norway. In brief, although the students in our case study meet in a number of one-week gatherings, there seemed to be a need for online socialization and trust building to succeed in regular group work collaboration. The study program uses a system of student evaluation that is portfolio-based, each portfolio consisting of several group assignments. Collaborative learning is a challenge in itself, and collaborative writing adds further challenges to the group process. Until that time students in the part-time program used a traditional online learning platform (Fronter) for distance collaboration, with asynchronous communication via discussion boards, online documents and e-mail. Our experience with distance education, and feedback from students, suggested that there was a need for more synchronous collaboration and a more continuous online learning community. These needs motive our research. This paper seeks to address the following exploratory research questions:

1. What do students experience as important preconditions for an online collaborative environment?
2. What features of virtual world technologies (e.g. Second Life) are needed to form a basis for a suitable social and communicative collaborative framework for distance learners?

The remaining paper is presented as follows. In the next section we clarify meaning of the concepts of collaboration and collaborative writing and we present prior research in this domain. In Section 3 we give a description of our theoretical framework for this project. In Section 4 we describe our data collection method. Section 5 offers analysis and discussion of the findings. Section 6 presents the implications and concluding remarks.

2   Literature Review

Research on collaborative writing often stresses support for the task of writing, at the expense of the communication and interaction which takes place during writing as argued in Mitchell [6], while Rimmershaw [7] allows for an emphasis on group dynamics. We define CW according to Lowry et al, as: "an iterative and social process that involves a team focused on a common objective that negotiates, coordinates and communicates during the creation of a common document" [8, p.72].

Brodahl [9] points out that true CW cannot be fully supported by collaborative tools alone, referring to Google Docs and EtherPad as examples. Dopke [10] is concerned with group communication as central to CW, and along with pre-collaboration planning and socializing. According to Kraut et al [11], CW requires that group members establish shared achievement goals and allocate roles within the group, including shared rhetorical goals are required, and shared understanding of the facts of the document.

Bjørn and Ngwenyama [12] address the complexity of building shared meaning when participants are geographically distributed. Particularly visibility is seen as essential to collaborative practices within virtual teams, where all participants are capable of observing each other's actions and social cues during the collaboration. This is considered to strengthen the accountability and awareness, and to hinder communication breakdowns.

In a much cited study by De Lucia et al [13] involving university students, they evaluate an online learning environment, designed for collaboration. The study shows that in a 3D multi-user virtual environment, Second Life, learning was strongly related to the user perception of belonging to a learning community, and also to the experience of awareness, presence and communication [15].

Daft and Lengel [14] propose that communication media have varying capacities for resolving ambiguity, negotiating varying interpretations, and facilitating understanding. They present a media richness hierarchy, with face-to-face communication on top, as the richest communication medium in the hierarchy, and that state that richer media provide more social cues, e.g. non-verbal communication, and are generally more effective for communication of equivocal issues than leaner, less rich media.

Saeed et al [15] find that Second Life (SL) is a highly rich medium, with it's ability to transmit multiple cues (graphics, voice, text, gestures). Their findings suggest that SL should be able to reduce uncertainty and equivocality of tasks, and therefore has the capacity to increase effective communication among its users. They have been criticized for being too simplified, e.g. it is argued that sometimes accuracy of communication is more important than richness [16], factors such as that users see technology ease of use as more important than media richness [17], and that distance learning through audio conferencing is as effective as face-to-face learning [18].

Although good media choice will be partly task and user dependent, there is still reason to believe that a sensory rich environment has potential to enhance team-building and cohesiveness [19], including non-verbal and relational cues in communication. Franceschi et al [20] argue that visually identifying collaborating parties affect the sense of belonging and trust, and helps in the group's management of roles and responsibilities. They emphasize the potential of VW's for the support of effective collaborative e-learning and state that other e-learning environments often do not provide sufficient support for group collaboration.

Davis et al [19] argues that VW's have the potential to simulate the experience of physical co-presence, which in turn is important for reaching similar levels of trust to that which occurs in face-to-face teams. Some studies also indicate that avatar-based interactions lead to greater experience of co-presence than interaction via other media, like for instance phone or text chat [21][22]. This may be partly due to a stronger sense of immersion in VW's [22], a concept often associated with presence.

Williams [23] elaborates on the role of trust in teams, described as the key feature for any type of team environment. He emphasizes the ways that virtual writing teams can build trust by using communication behaviours to demonstrate shared understanding. He argues that the concept of social presence contains important aspects for overcoming the problems of virtual teams. Social presence is about the experience of "being there together", a feeling of actually meeting each other. The avatars of 3D VW's enable nonverbal cues that strengthen this feeling, such as proximity and gestures. The author also emphasizes the importance of frequent and explicit communication, and to accomplish tasks in an effective and predictive way, for building trust in virtual teams.

Another factor that has been given much attention is the role of informal interaction in building trust. Broady [24] argues that trust comes partially through informal contact, and that informal contact can be stimulated by appropriate tools. In co-located teams the social or relational part of interpersonal communication comes nearly instinctively. Not so with virtual teams, where informal contact has to be stimulated specifically. Informal contact in virtual collaboration settings strengthens and deepens relationships between the individuals involved [24] [25]. The frequently cited work by Jarvenpaa and Leiduer [26] also emphasizes informal contact, more specifically called social (non-task) communication. They found that extensive social communication appeared to foster trust in the initial phases of a project, but was insufficient in maintaining trust in the long run. Task-oriented communication seems to become increasingly important over time, regarding building and maintaining trust. This includes establishing a predictable communication pattern.

The main purpose of our study is to shed light on design considerations that are important for designing a virtual collaboration environment for distance learners. In this regard, we will draw on a multi-functional model of group process and development, described in the next section.

3   Theoretical Framework

Joseph McGrath's [27] theoretical framework Time-Interaction-Performance (TIP) is about temporal processes in group interaction and performance, hence TIP, for short. His goal is to conceptualize groups and group activity in a way that reflects the processes of naturally occurring groups, as we meet them in our everyday lives. The TIP model treats groups dynamically and takes into account the physical, temporal, and social context which the groups are a part of and emphasizes temporal patterning of interaction and performance in such groups.

Fundamental to the structure of the TIP model is the multiple functions of groups, associated with contributions groups make to systems on three levels: externally, to systems the group is a part of; internally, to the individuals constituting the group, and also internally to the group as a whole. McGrath calls these functions the group's production function, member-support function, and group well-being function, respectively [27]. He states that a group at any time will be engaged in activities having to do with all three functions. All groups therefore have to find ways to coordinate multiple functions, overlapping in time, space and members. McGrath points out this parallel and builds on the theories of several others, including group effectiveness [28] and group dimensions [29].

The other dimension in the TIP model consists of four modes of group activity that transcend the various group functions. According to McGrath modes are potential, not required, forms of activity; although all group action involves one or another of the four modes of group activity:

Mode I: inception and acceptance of a project (goal choice),
Mode II: problem solving provision of solution to technical issues (means choice),
Mode III: conflict resolution, that is, of political issues (policy choice), and
Mode IV: execution of performance requirements of the project (goal attainment).

The modes are akin to what is often referred to as problem-solving phases, and reflects the relation between the group and the environment within which the group is operating. In Section 5, we interpret our findings through the theoretical lens of TIP, focusing on how the groups mobilize different functions to meet the challenges of online collaboration.

4   Method

This study was undertaken using participants from a part-time bachelor program of Social Education at Molde University College in Norway. The students in the program live geographically dispersed, and meet in one-week gatherings two or three times per semester, in addition to some face-to-face group meetings. The Social Education study program had 45 part-time students. The majority of the students were in the age group of 35 to 50, and earlier assessment of ICT capabilities indicated moderate to low competence level. Two of seven student groups, each of seven to nine students, were selected to try out certain aspects of collaboration and writing in a VW environment. Two groups were selected for this study based on their choice to join. In addition, project groups were selected on the basis of requirements for computer equipment, meaning that all members of the group had computers and Internet access from their home that would address SL system requirements. Participation in this project would count as part of the students normal group work. Student groups were neither rewarded nor penalized for participating in the project. The two selected groups would receive training in how to use the selected VW, Second Life. In total, 16 students entered SL and were active in the virtual world for this project.

In the spring of 2011, the project period was divided into three learning cycles with associated learning goals, each lasting about three to four weeks. Thereafter a fourth evaluative cycle used the qualitative method of Focus group interview [30]. The main themes and learning goals of the three first cycles were respectively: communication, collaboration and collaborative writing. The project leader offered continual training and guidance during the process, in SL and by phone. In Cycle 1, communication, the emphasis was on learning the technology and software, on getting started with voice chat and text chat, and finally on mutual verbal dialogue in SL. In this cycle the dialogue was connected to a small group assignment about disability, challenging the project groups to communicate via SL. In Cycle 2, collaboration, dialogue was still important, but now the focus was on learning and trying out the basics of virtual interaction and socialization, necessary for teamwork. In this cycle the collaboration was connected to various preparations for an upcoming exam, which required a range of forms of collaboration, from collecting, sharing and discussion of information, to relational support and encouragement. In Cycle 3, collaborative writing, the emphasis was on trying out writing collaboratively, preferably inside of SL using Google Docs (GD), a web-based CW tool. In this cycle the writing was connected to a portfolio assignment about group rules, evaluation and revision regarding the upcoming third year of the program. In Cycle 4 focus group interviews were conducted based on the research questions.

In accordance with our iterative design, data collection took place both during and after the project. Along the way, the project leader engaged in unstructured conversation with the participants, in conjunction with the training and guidance. This provided feedback on the strengths and weaknesses of the procedures, relevant for considering necessary course corrections. After completing Cycle 3, focus group interviews based on the research questions were used to obtain students' experiences. The interviews were conducted by an interview moderator and a note taker. The project leader was not present in the focus group interviews. Partly because of the size of the groups, interviews were conducted with group members mixed randomly into three new groups, each of five to six members. In addition to voice recordings of the entire interviews, a log was written during the process.

Qualitative analysis procedures were conducted using descriptive content analysis [31], identifying criteria for CW in SL. The identified criteria were categorized into themes and patterns, and given a theory-guided coding, elaborated below. Excel was used for analysis of the transcribed interview data. Transcripts and results were reviewed by the first author, supporting validity of content analysis.

The second author read the transcripts and coded them in two ways – according to the modes and functions of McGrath's TIP theory, and according to three concepts central to SL research – presence, awareness and belonging. The second author made notes about patterns in the data, and emerging content themes. The two authors read the transcripts together and discussed the second author's interpretations. In this discussion, the authors considered the levels of consistency, frequency, extensiveness and intensity among the participants [30]. A summary of the interpretations was sent to four of the participants, randomly chosen, which were invited to provide comments and corrections to the interpretation. The participants reported that they considered the summary as sensible and recognizable, and supported in this way the validity of the interpretations.

5   TIP Analysis and Discussion

Based on data from the focus group interviews, modes and functions of student group interaction were analyzed using TIP theory [27]. The findings were compared to feedback received from the groups during the project. We provide a few quotes and references from participants in this section to demonstrate the validity of the analysis. For further information on the dataset the reader is referred the authors.

In the **Inception Mode I**, the group members were choosing and adjusting goals, in accordance with characteristics of framework conditions as well as characteristics and ambitions of the group members themselves. Our focus group interviews show that, in spite of a general positive attitude to participating in the project, many participants did experience difficulties in giving it a high priority, in a semester with several important exams.

Some of the students struggled with technical difficulties, mainly with the voice chat function. Together with experiences of time pressure and limited ICT skills, it is likely that these challenges affected the achievement level of many of the participants

[9]. However, there were also considerable individual differences in achievement level, and some of the students had clear expectations for communicating and collaborating in a VW (Participant 15).

At a cognitive level the group members needed to establish shared rhetorical goals [11]. These are content-oriented goals, and may be divided into two variations: product goals and process goals. As intended, product goals played a minor role in this exploring project, but the assignments were authentic and equal for all students in the part-time program. Because of the upcoming exams the students were always free to work and collaborate in alternative ways when needed. The process goals of communication, collaboration and collaborative writing were stressed by the project leader, through continuous guidance and supervision.

Although the students knew each other before the project, the early stages of the project were expected to be important for online socialization and trust building [32]. And the findings suggest that the participants experienced more immersion and presence [19] in SL than their ICT skills, expectations and choice of goals would indicate: "I knew of course that there were several who had hardly touched a computer ... And now they're using Second Life, with all its challenges. And they have mastered it! So I think, in fact, it's ... hugely impressive." (Participant 6).

It is interesting to note that in spite of a well-known steep learning curve in SL [19], many of the comments show clear indications of well-being in the groups, in the early phases of in-world socialization: "What I think was nice, is that we have laughed a lot inside there (SL). Lots of good humor... And that we discovered new sides of each other, after several years of collaboration. For example, Z, when she arrives with that handbag, on her avatar bike, and then she starts to dance! ...We let ourselves go a little inside there, and it helped to create a good feeling - inside Second Life." (Participant 13).

In summary of this phase of the project most of the participants chose sets of interaction opportunities involving informal and off-topic contact/communication, probably important for building and maintaining trust in the groups [24].

During the **problem solving Mode II** group members were choosing means, both practical and interpersonal, that included how to involve all members and allow them to share their competencies in the collaboration. In this case study the students relied heavily on voice chat for communication, and when problems arose with sound, some of the students felt they lost contact with the group. Although different students dropped out from time to time, it did something with the inclusion in the group process: "The experience of falling out, and having to use text chat to get in contact again – it was terrible. (Others nod and say "yes".) You really feel left out. You see and hear that the others are in contact, but they don't hear you. You are on the outside." (Participant 4)

Using text chat felt like a bad option, according to the students, and was only used when necessary. This may partly have to do with expectations, but Sallnäs [33] found that people do not perceive themselves to be virtually present when communicating through text-chat, compared to voice-chat. In a study of collaborative problem-solving, Reimann and Zumbach [34] characterized text-based communication as a comparatively poor medium, pointing specifically to its ability to support the three functions described in TIP theory. Because the students did not see text chat as an alternative to voice chat, this sometimes had an exasperating effect on group communications and affected the group process quite a bit. In response, the project leader decided to introduce another tool for voice chat – called TinyChat (TC) [35]. Very few of the participants had difficulties learning to use TC, and it turned out to be a stable solution for voice, when communicating in SL. Some students even reported as having their best user experience in SL in this phase of the project – that is after introducing TC, and before starting to write collaboratively.

When Google Docs (GD) was introduced for CW, this turned out to be promising, but also a new challenge. A new technical problem occurred – GD did not function as expected inside of SL, and often did not appear on screen in the SL classroom. It varied from time to time who had the problem viewing shared documents, but nevertheless it hindered the groups as a whole, when trying to write collaboratively inside of SL. Since CW played an important role in the study, the project leader decided to let the students write in GD outside of SL. The implications of this were both negative and positive. The students now had to manage three program interfaces at once – SL, TC and GD, for meeting, talking and writing, respectively. This was a minimal functioning solution, but happened to be "too much", both for the students and some of their laptops as some started to overheat: "We were dependent on using TinyChat for communication and Google Docs for collaborative writing, so - - we ended up quitting Second Life. The combination of programs also exceeds the capacity of your computer." (Participant 6) On the other hand, the students experienced the combination of GD and TC as very promising, and these tools therefore dominated their choice of means for the writing phase. We were thus left with two separate and unlike periods of the project, both in which the students reported a good amount of well-being: A period using the combination of SL and TC, and a period using the combination of GD and TC. The planned combination of SL and GD did not function as expected, or was not accepted by the students.

In **conflict resolution Mode III** the production function is a political preference resolving mode – attempts to resolve potentially conflicting preferences, values, or interests within the group. As a part of a community of practice [3] group members will exchange and negotiate on ideas, meanings and knowledge, and through this develop a common platform for the group. The students had very few reports on open conflicts in the groups, but there were still some signs of frustration and resistance: "Not everyone in our group wanted to participate in the SL project, but our group rules tell us that the majority decides." (Participant 7).

This may be part of the explanation for why the groups chose to downgrade SL, after repeated negotiations within the groups, and to go for the combination of TC and GD only. In Mode III the well-being function involves power and payoff allocation, and the member support function is about individual's expected contributions to and payoff from the group's purposeful activities.

Distribution of roles in SL was a recurring theme among the students in this study, although the participants did not seem to find fully satisfactory solutions. Who should lead, and who should talk, when and about what? They perceived the groups as large, maybe too large for effective communication in a VW:"...and it is even worse when 9 people are talking at once, and are not getting heard. In the end perhaps half of the group is saying nothing." (Participant 3) "Currently we are not disciplined enough to be that many in SL simultaneously. In that case we should have had some sound or sign ... (showing who will talk)." (Participant 7) It is possible that the phasing out of SL functioned as a kind of conflict resolution, since the experiences were contradictory. Some obviously felt rather immersed in SL in spite of the challenges: "What I was saying... you feel you are there. You get a presence. Although there are a couple of things missing, of course, ... gestures, etc. But nevertheless, I feel that I am there, in a way. It's just the way avatars are – I know the avatar is B, and I feel that when I look at that avatar, it's her." (Participant 16).

Summarizing the third phase, students received support to focus on exam preparations when in conflict with project tasks. Although the groups as a whole stopped using SL for group writing tasks, some subgroups still used it from time to time, for discussion and social contact. This probably was due to both their individual relationship to SL, and to communicational and technical challenges related to larger groups.

In **execution Mode IV** of the TIP model, the so-called production function is about behaviors associated with goal attainment, in this case primarily meaning the process goal of CW. The other functions in this mode, concerning interaction and participation, are associated with the sub-goals of communication and collaboration. The main goal of CW was attained using GD, and after a period of communicating and collaborating in SL. However, the groups did not succeed in using GD and SL simultaneously, and the writing was not executed on screen in SL. Most of the students characterized GD as a great tool for CW, in combination with TC for sound: "We have the same experience in our group ... The sound in Second Life did not work so well. So therefore we use Google Docs, and TinyChat as well - in combination. That's when we have the best outcomes." (Participant 2) The reason why GD was so well received probably had to do with an increased experience of awareness and overview in relation to what the others did and had done in the writing process [36] [13] (Participant 6).

As we have seen, the experience of presence in VW is thought to be essential because of its potential for facilitating collaboration [37] [38]. Presence also is likely to foster engagement and trust [39] in the group, which in mode IV is relevant for both well-being function and member support. The well-being function in this case is about conducting interpersonal interaction needed for task performance, while member support in this mode is about members' concrete participation in the group's activities. In the stages prior to CW several students experienced strong feelings of presence and immersion (Participant 16). These kinds of experiences may also indicate a sense of belonging to a community [13]. Other participants emphasized the importance of informal interaction in SL, and how it establishes a good atmosphere for collaboration: "When we had group meetings there were different places where we could meet - e.g. around a campfire... It was nice, when we sat around the campfire... Y with her feet on the table – in a relaxed position, informal – but still discussing formal topics." (Participant 13) In addition, the experiences might contribute to an awareness of each other's activities, positions and degree of formality [36], important in building trust and shared understanding in groups.

The need to "visualize" other people's activities as a context for their own activities (i.e. awareness) may be one reason why some saw a potential in SL as an arena for CW: "Now, if the technical issues are solved, I very strongly believe in meeting in Second Life, in a meeting room, and writing collaboratively on a screen. Because of the way we are distributed geographically, this is a great opportunity. Being able to sit like we do, discuss stuff and have a big screen that we can write on together. I believe in this." (Participant 2).

Beyond the point about being able to meet, discuss and write within the same application, not many of the students elaborated specifically on the benefits of SL vs. TC as a social and communicative framework for CW. However, it was commented on the importance of being able to see visual representations of each other when communicating: "... I see that it (SL) can be used for discussions. To get this group feeling – of being in a group, sitting and talking. This is because I feel it is nice to have something to fix my eyes on. When using TinyChat - where do you fix your eyes? I think it has something to do with cohesion, when you sit and talk in Second Life ... instead of having only TinyChat." (Participant 16).

According to the literature, cohesion and other indications of social presence are important preconditions for CW [40][10]. Informal interaction and socializing also seem to be an important basis for CW [8][36][41], which was experienced, by the majority of our participants in SL. At the same time many participants missed more detailed visual body signals in SL, which they felt would have facilitated more meaningful nonverbal communication: "(Using SL) you are able to collaborate at a distance ... (geographic) boundaries become less important. Personally I'm still fonder of meeting people physically; being able to look them in their face, see their expression. You lose that in Second Life. I think this is a great loss, because this is what makes us human." (Participant 13).

When asked about the role of SL in CW, most of the students' "blamed the technology" for their frustrations: "One thing is if we had not made it (managing Second Life)... but we actually mastered it. It was the technical problems that hindered us. I think everyone has seen the possibilities in there, seen the positive in Second Life, the way it was meant to be used. But when half of the teamwork time is spent on getting it to work, then there will be huge frustration ..." (Participant 6). Other participants identified technology problems as: a need for more training and guidance, and the downsides of using laptops, which often got very warm using SL.

Some studies note choosing alternative VW technologies to SL with the most important reason was increased workload because of SL's steep learning curve [42]. Other reasons included more general time pressure and concerns about instability of the learning environment, such as downtime, access and maneuvering concerns in SL. Alrayes and Sutcliffe [43] found that students did not prefer SL over traditional ways of group working, in spite of positive motivation using the VW. The authors suggest that this may be due to poor usability, and that SL was not familiar to the participants. Nevertheless, we found clear individual differences in our study, and some students even said that they felt connected and "inside" in spite of losing audio connection with the group. Some comments could indicate age and competence dependent reactions to SL: "Some of us had to go on courses to learn how to find the on-and-off button, right. I think that – young people, they have a lot of experience with computers, and look at computers as tools. They learn it so much easier." (Participant 7).

Table 1 summarizes some of the key findings in light of TIP theory, illustrating how the groups mobilize different functions in varying modes. For clarification, "revision of the means choice" is part of the technical problem solving phase that focused on the changing the way the group chose to solve the technical problems. The "position of involvement" describes the status of the member support in the problem solving phase. In phase 3, "differing interests" refers to policy used in conflict resolution, and "roles" refers to the role of power distribution within the group in conflict resolution. Also in phase 3, "negotiation" refers to the possible payoff relationships as they contributed to conflict resolution. Following TIP theory the steps between modes in our case study seem to take a "satisficing" path to execution.

Table 1. The groups' mobilization of different functions in varying modes

Functions:	Production	Well-being	Member support
M **o** **d** **e** **s** I:Inception	**Process goal -** The process goal of CW inside of SL was chosen by the project management, but later modified in agreement with the participants	**Informal Interaction-** The students were engaged in informal interaction during the initial socialization [32] in SL, and many experienced immersion and presence	**Achievement Level -** There were individual differences in terms of achievement level in relation to the project
II: **Problem solving**	**Revision of the means choice-** Problems with GD on screen in SL opened for testing GD outside of SL, and eventually independent of SL	**Role of Communication -** Voice chat was seen as essential for communication, and some students experienced their best period in SL using Tiny Chat	**Position of Involvement -** Issues with voice chat in SL made some participants feel left out, and only a few felt that text chat contributed to involvement
III: **Conflict resolution**	**Differing Interests** - The students were given freedom in relation to the use of SL, which may have functioned as conflict prevention	**Roles -** The groups struggled with the moderator role and other roles in SL, and pointed to limited opportunities for nonverbal communication in SL	**Negotiation -** Frustration over technical issues became a challenge to collaboration, and required recurring negotiations on ambitions and strategies
IV: **Execution**	**Collaborative writing -** Participants had feelings of overview "seeing the big picture" and awareness when collaborating in GD, they knew the other's "state" in the writing process	**Collaboration -** Early interaction in SL may have fostered later collaboration, contributing to feelings of presence, awareness and belonging	**Participation -** Most of the students actively participated in the execution phase, after a period of variable participation

6   Implications and Conclusion

We used McGrath's TIP theory [27] to examine the question, what do students experience as important preconditions for an online collaborative environment. To do so we examined group processes related to online group work and CW task in a part-time education program. In case design and our analysis it was assumed that negotiation of meaning is central in the CW task. We concluded, a good negotiation climate must build on already established online communication and collaboration in the group, which includes experience of presence, awareness and belonging to the group. This again depends upon efficient tools for communication and collaboration.

Addressing the second research question our study explored what are some the features of VW technologies needed to form a basis for suitable social and communicative collaboration. In summary, we found the technical challenges made it difficult to try out CW in SL, and student experiences therefore divided into two main types: a) experiences with CW in GD, which generally were very good, and b) experiences with communication and collaboration in SL, which were more mixed, and best after introduction of TC for voice chat. The size of the groups clearly became an extra challenge to the communication. Many participants experienced too many challenges with SL to want to continue using it. Others saw a clear potential in CW on screen in SL, perhaps because they experienced a stronger social presence and awareness in SL, which we know is also important for CW.

In summary, the students gave many positive descriptions of experiences in SL that we consider VW's as promising learning arenas. Several students also seemed to handle the technical challenges well; they looked for solutions and maintained motivation. At the same time there is no doubt that the technical issues were serious obstacles in this study, and have to be dealt with in future selection of technologies or design of VW environments. There is a need for more stable solutions, and better integration of CW tools in the VW environments.

Our focus group interviews had shown individual differences regarding user evaluation of SL, while collaborative writing in GD and TC were almost unanimously positive described by participants. The impression is that younger people with average to good ICT skills seem to benefit the most from collaboration in a VW environment. At the same time it is likely that better training and supervision may raise student's tolerance for technical problems. It is also possible that individuals with a visual perceptual style may have greater outcomes than those with a more auditory style. Some participants emphasized the benefits of seeing the visual interaction and body language of the participants, while others emphasized voice chat as sufficient. The question is whether these differences would be as great if the students had not known each other from earlier face-to-face collaboration.

When it comes to awareness, students described collaboration on the CW task in GD as unifying and raising awareness, and emphasized how important it is to know the others "state" in the writing process, meaning that they know who is writing what, when and where, which makes it easier to work together in an integrated way. Awareness, in this context, probably has both a task-oriented and relational side. The task-oriented side is about overview and understanding of each other's academic activities, real and potential, at various points in the writing process [36][44]. Relational awareness, or social awareness is about overview of each other's social roles in a workflow, where e.g. motivation, initiative and so on will have an impact on how to collaborate in the writing process. Being together in the same virtual space seems to increase social awareness, probably through perceptions of co-presence with others [46]. One surprising finding is that the SL experience may have increased social awareness of the group that could have resulted in a stronger positive experience of CW in GD than what might have occurred in absence of the SL experience phase. According to Prasalova-Forland [45] CW tools do not always provide sufficient awareness about social roles and relationships, known as essential for group learning. In other words, the positive experience with GD may not have been as positive without the prior "socialization" phase in SL. This concurs with Salmon [32] that also points out as a necessary step in online learning.

We recognize a limitation of this study is based on our qualitative approach. That it is not possible to express in quantitative terms, of "how much" importance the VW environment experience have been for social awareness in our study and "how much" this may have influenced the positive experience of CW in GD. The students already knew each other before the study, from two years of collaboration, and may have felt a limited need for socialization. Nevertheless, we find it likely that social awareness requires continuous maintenance and also that virtual collaboration to some degree requires virtual awareness, based on the experiences made through virtual social interaction.

In conclusion, the extent of importance of the role VW environments in relation to collaboration in the case of CW seems to be both phase dependent (e.g. socialization needs) and task dependent (e.g. degree of equivocality). However, our research concurs with McGrath's in that social functions of group well-being and member support are potentially important in all phases of collaboration. As we saw in our study, on some occasions participants chose to meet in the VW during the writing phase of the project, when needing informal discussion and negotiation of meaning. In answer to the research question 1, these students indicated that the VW environment was a good arena for shared reflection and for dialogue about complex issues.

An ancillary finding drawn from this study is that students experienced and valued learning skills in a domain that was outside of their primary academic domain as Social Educators. The majority of the students were older, second career students. Interviews with them provided us with rich descriptive evidence that VW environments such as SL are fun and immersive. Many reported that the experience increased their self confidence and feelings of competency in dealing with VW technologies. The students also described experiences of presence, awareness and belonging – important for the building of trust, negotiation of meaning and collaborative writing. These findings suggest that such potential may increase as virtual worlds become more sophisticated with regard to visual cues and nonverbal communication and that through support of socialization provide a good basis for collaboration. The growing need to communicate and learn at a distance, should also inspire future exploratory research of how virtual world technologies can be applied to achieve more effective and improved collaboration for distance learners.

References

1. Vygotsky, L.: Mind in society: the development of higher psychological processes. Harvard University Press, Cambridge (1978)
2. Erkens, G., Jaspers, J., Prangsma, M., Kanselaar, G.: Coordination processes in computer supported collaborative writing. Computers in Human Behavior 21, 463–486 (2005)
3. Wenger, E.: Communities of practice. Learning, meaning, and identity. Cambridge University Press, Cambridge (1998)
4. Bjorn, P., Scupola, A., Fitzgerald, B.: Expanding Technological Frames towards Mediated Collaboration. Scandinavian Journal of Information Systems 18(2), 28–47 (2007)
5. Parker, K.R., Chao, J.T.: Wiki as a teaching tool. Interdisciplinary Journal of Knowledge and Learning Objects 3, 57–72 (2007)
6. Mitchell, A.: Communication and Shared Understanding in Collaborative Writing. Master's Thesis, Department of Computer Science, University of Toronto (1996), http://www.ufrgs.br/limc/escritacoletiva/pdf/com_and_shared_understand.pdf (retrieved November 13, 2012)
7. Rimmershaw, R.: Collaborative Writing Practices and Writing Support Technologies. Instructional Science 21, 15–28 (1992)
8. Lowry, P.B., Curtis, A., Lowry, M.R.: Building a taxonomy and nomenclature of collaborative writing to improve interdisciplinary research and practice. Journal of Business Communication 41, 66–99 (2004)
9. Brodahl, C., Hadjerrouit, S., Hansen, N.K.: Collaborative Writing with Web 2.0 Technologies: Education Students' Perceptions. Journal of Information Technology Education: Innovations in Practice 10, 73–103 (2011)
10. Dopke, L.: An Exploration of Communication Strategies for Effectively Organizing and Managing Collaborative Grant Writing Groups. Masters theses, Graduate Faculty of Grand Valley State University (2011)
11. Kraut, R., Galegher, J., Fish, R., Chalfonte, B.: Task Requirements and Media Choice in Collaborative Writing. Human-Computer Interaction 7(4), 375–407 (1992)
12. Bjørn, P., Ngwenyama, O.: Virtual team collaboration: building shared meaning, resolving breakdowns and creating translucence. Information Systems Journal 19(3), 227–253 (2009)
13. De Lucia, A.D., Francese, R., Passero, I., Tortora, G.: Development and evaluation of a virtual campus on Second Life: The case of SecondDMI. Computers & Education 52(1), 220–233 (2009)
14. Daft, R.L., Lengel, R.H.: Organizational information requirements, media richness, and structural design. Journal of Management Science 32(5), 554–571 (1996)
15. Saeed, N., Yang, Y., Sinnappan, S.: Media richness and user acceptance of Second Life. In: Proceedings of Ascilite, Melbourne (2008)
16. Dennis, A., Valacich, J., Speier, C., Morris, M.: Beyond media richness: an empirical test of Media Synchronicity Theory. In: Proceedings of the 30th Hawaii International Conference on System Sciences, pp. 1060–1125 (1998)
17. Baninajarian, N., Abdullah, Z., Bolong, J.: The role of email in improving task performance among the executives in Malaysia. Australian Journal of Business and Management Research 1(4), 52–62 (2011)
18. Blau, I., Caspi, A.: Do media richness and visual anonymity influence learning? A comparative study using Skype. In: Eshet, Y., Caspi, A., Geri, N. (eds.) Learning in the Technological Era, pp. 18–25. The Open University of Israel, Ra'anana (2008)

19. Davis, A., Murphy, J., Owens, D., Khazanchi, D., Zigurs, I.: Avatars, people, and virtual worlds: Foundations for research in metaverses. Journal of the Association for Information Systems 10(2), 90–117 (2009)

20. Franceschi, K., Lee, R., Hinds, D.: Engaging elearning in virtual worlds: Supporting group collaboration. In: Proceedings of the 41st Annual Hawaii International Conference on System Sciences (2008)

21. Bente, G., Ruggenberg, S., Kramer, N.C., Eschenburg, F.: Avatar-mediated networking: Increasing social presence and interpersonal trust in net-based collaborations. Human Communication Research 34, 287–318 (2008)

22. Khan, S.: Sarah & Emma: Case studies of two instructors and how they use social presence in second life. Doctor of Philosophy. Texas State University, San Marcos (2011), https://digital.library.txstate.edu/bitstream/handle/10877/2 411/KHAN-DISSERTATION.pdf?sequence=1 (retrieved June 9, 2012)

23. Williams, S.D.: Forming Trust in Virtual Writing Teams: Perspectives and Applications. In: Hewett, B.L., Robidoux, C. (eds.) Virtual Collaborative Writing in the Workplace: Computer-Mediated Communication Technologies and Processes, Hershey, New York, pp. 88–111 (2010)

24. Broady, A.F.: Informal collaboration tools for global software development teams. Developer Works, IBM (2009), http://www.ibm.com/developerworks/rational/library/09/inform alcollaborationtoolsforglobalsoftwaredevelopmentteams/index. html (retrieved 2012)

25. Wojahn, P., Blicharz, K., Taylor, S.: Engaging in Virtual Collaborative Writing: Issues, Obstacles, and Strategies. In: Hewett, B., Robidoux, C. (eds.) Virtual Collaborative Writing in the Workplace: Computer-Mediated Communication Technologies and Processes, pp. 65–87. Hershey, New York (2010)

26. Jarvenpaa, S.L., Leidner, D.E.: Communication and trust in global virtual teams. Organization Science 10(6), 791–815 (1999)

27. McGrath, J.E.: Time Interaction Performance (TIP): A Theory of Groups. Small Group Research 22(2), 147–174 (1991)

28. Hackman, J.R.: Doing research that makes a difference. In: Lawler, E.E., Mohrman, A.M., Mohrman, S.A., Ledford, G.E., Cummings, T.G. (eds.) Doing Research that is Useful for Theory and Practice. Jossey-Bass, San Francisco (1985)

29. Bales, R.F.: The Equilibrium Problem in Small Groups. In: Parsons, T., Bales, R.F., Shils, E.A. (eds.) Working Papers in the Theory of Action. Free Press, Glencoe (1953)

30. Krueger, R.A.: Focus groups: A practical guide for applied research, 2nd edn. SAGE (1994)

31. Patton, M.Q.: Qualitative research and evaluation methods, 3rd edn. Sage Publications, Thousand Oaks (2002)

32. Salmon, G.: E-moderating: The key to teaching and learning online. Kogan Page Limited, London (2000)

33. Sallnäs, E.: Collaboration in multimodal virtual worlds: Comparing touch, text, voice and video. In: Schroeder, R. (ed.) Social Life of Avatars, pp. 172–187. Springer, Heidelberg (2002)

34. Reimann, P., Zumbach, J.: Supporting virtual learning teams with dynamic feedback. In: Lee, K.T., Mitchell, K. (eds.) The "Second Wave" of ICT in Education: From Facilitating Teaching and Learning to Engendering Education Reform, pp. 424–430. AACE, Hong Kong (2003)

35. Burns, M.: Distance education for teacher training: Modes, models and methods. Education Development Center, Washington (2011)
36. Dourish, P., Bellotti, V.: Awareness and coordination in shared workspaces. In: Proceedings of CSCW 1992, pp. 197–214 (1992)
37. Dickey, M.D.: Three-dimensional virtual worlds and distance learning: two case studies of Active Worlds as a medium for distance education. British Journal of Educational Technology 36(3), 439–451 (2005)
38. Franceschi-Diaz, K.G.: Group presence in virtual worlds: Supporting collaborative e-learning. ProQuest ETD Collection for FIU. Paper AAI3377921 (2009), http://digitalcommons.fiu.edu/dissertations/AAI3377921 (retrieved June 2, 2012)
39. Gunawardena, C.N., Nolla, A.C., Wilson, P.L., Lopez-Islas, J.R., Ramirez-Angel, N., Megchun-Alpizar, R.M.: A Cross-Cultural Study of Group Process and Development in Online Conferences. Distance Education 22(1), 85–121 (2001)
40. Stanek, O.: Towards a Collaborative Meeting Environment in a Virtual World. Master thesis, University of Zurich, Faculty of Economics (2008), http://www.ifi.uzh.ch/pax/uploads/pdf/publication/677/Diplom arbeit_Oliver_Stanek.pdf (retrieved 2012)
41. Andersen, R., Robidoux, C.: Building a collaborative writing strategy. Best Practices 13, 61–70 (2011), http://www.infomanagementcenter.com/members/pdfs/reprints/BP 2011-06Andersen_Robidoux.pdf
42. Gütl, C., Chang, V., Kopeinik, S., Williams, R.: 3D virtual worlds as a tool for collaborative learning settings in geographically dispersed environments. In: Auer, M. (ed.) 12th International Conference on Interactive Computer Aided Learning, pp. 310–323. International Association of Online Engineering, Villach (2009)
43. Alrayes, A., Sutcliffe, A.: Students' attitudes in a virtual environment (SecondLife). Journal of Virtual Worlds Research 4(1), 1–17 (2011)
44. Eklundh, S.: Supporting Individual Views and Mutual Awareness in a Collaborative Writing Task: The Case of Collaboracio. In: Galbraith, D.W. (ed.) Writing and Cognition. Studies in Writing, vol. 20, pp. 323–334. Emerald Group Publishing Limited (2007)
45. Prasolova-Førland, E.: Supporting social awareness among university students in 3D CVEs: Benefits and limitations. In: Proceedings of the Third International Conference on Cyberworlds, pp. 127–134 (2004)
46. Wigert, B., Vreede, G., Boughzala, I., Bououd, I.: Collaboration in Virtual Worlds: The Role of the Facilitator. In: Hawaii international Conference on System Sciences 2012, pp. 973–982, (2012)

Architecting in Large and Complex Information Infrastructures

Olav Poppe, Johan Sæbø, and Petter Nielsen

University of Oslo, Department of Informatics,
Postboks 1080 Blindern, 0316 Oslo, Norway
{olavpo,johansa,pnielsen}@ifi.uio.no

Abstract. This paper is based on a critical perspective on the coordination of information systems in the health sector in developing countries. Two stories of health information system implementations in West Africa are presented. These are stories of integration, interoperability and architecting processes unfolding in a space where different actors pursue different and often conflicting agendas and where power and politics are at play. Our point of departure is an understanding of information systems as information infrastructures, being large scale, complex, and evolving over time. Our analysis of architecting large and complex information systems contributes to an understanding of information system architectures as a process. We argue that information system architecture is not simply made on the drawing board, but are the outcome of negotiations among actors about the division of labour, or role-making and role-taking, within the information infrastructure.

Keywords: Architecture, information infrastructure, health information systems.

1   Introduction

Health represents a complex domain, being intrinsically fragmented and compartmentalized due to a high level of specialization [1,2]. Health Information Systems have thus typically grown around supporting particular health services, with little thought for the overall system design. In developing countries, one of many additional factors has been the influence of the international health organizations, themselves often fragmented and acting in an autonomous manner. As a result, Health Information Systems (HIS) in developing countries are commonly tainted by fragmentation and uncoordinated development, severely restricting the ability to effectively manage health services [3]. As a consequence of the fragmentation, data collection is duplicated, information is not available in a timely fashion, if at all, to those who can make use of it, and already limited resources are spread thinly over many overlapping sub-systems. To deal with this critical situation, there is an increasing focus on the construction of holistic architectural frameworks for HIS, integrating disparate systems using standards for interoperability [4,5,6]. So far, these attempts have had little if any effect, an issue of urgent importance during the recent ebola outbreak in West Africa, which went to the core of the activities this paper

T.H. Commisso et al. (Eds.): SCIS 2014, LNBIP 186, pp. 90–104, 2014.

describes. The outbreak, which started in Guinea, quickly spread both within the country and to neighbouring countries, with the epicentre at the borders of Guinea, Sierra Leone, and Liberia. This highlighted a need not just for well functioning national HIS, but for a regional architectural framework which could support cross-border measures. Our research reports also from this work.

This paper is based on a critical perspective on the coordination of information systems in the health sector in developing countries. Based on a belief in the importance of information to support decision making, it tells a story of the development of HIS in West Africa. This is a story about coordination, but not as a centralized, formal and top-down approach. This story is about integration, interoperability and architecting as processes unfolding in a space where different actors pursue different and often conflicting agendas and where power and politics indeed are at play. Coordination is thus not primarily about specifying the perfect standard or drawing the perfect architecture. While standards and architectures are important, the most urgent challenge is seemingly to make and take roles and agree and maintain a common understanding of the borders between them.

This story of coordination is analysed as an architectural process, and as such relates to our current understanding and use of architecture within the field of information systems (IS), a use that is arguably incoherent and abstract. Taking as a point of departure an understanding of IS as information infrastructures (II), being large scale, complex, and evolving over time, analysing this case of architecting large and complex information systems in terms of role-making, role-taking and distribution of responsibilities will contribute to the understanding of information system architectures as a process. The focus will thus be on the when, where, and how it evolves, rather than just what it is.

2   Related Literature

In this section we present research on architecture and the process of architecting in the Information Systems literature. The concept has seen a rise of interest in recent years, but still appears theoretically immature, which is discussed below. Then we define our analytical lens as information infrastructures (II), which we see as useful in highlighting the complexities and socio-technical nature of the cases this paper discusses.

2.1   Architecture and Architecting in IS

We take as a point of departure the literature on architecture in the field of Information Systems (IS). Architecture has been applied in a variety of different ways, with a focus ranging from purely technical to more organizational aspects of IS [7,8]. While there seems to be a common understanding that it is a description of a system's components and their relationships, reflected in both definitions of the more technical and the more organizational flavours, it is often used in an abstract [6], or even usefully ambiguous way [9]. Traditionally, architecture has been applied to software, where it has been linked to design principles such as loose coupling and modularization. It is still extensively used for the organization of software, but has also more recently seen an influence from more organizational applications of the term, such as enterprise architecture. As a result, IS practitioners and researches alike have started to talk about different layers of architecture [10].

While the various layers of architecture are interlinked, their focuses have different implications. Scheil Corneliussen notes that an enterprise architecture approach take the context of the IT application more into account, and is less interested in the structure of the application itself [11].

Further, we see as a main deficiency in the IS literature on architecture the relative lack of understanding of architecting as a process, or how the architecture is created. The focus in the literature is on the architectural drawings or snapshots, rather than on the process leading there, giving the impression that architecture is an analytic problem to be solved on the architect's drawing board [10]. For example, the TOGAF architecture framework (as an emerging industry standard) does include guidelines to manage the building and evolution of architectures[1], but it has been critiqued as being too generic [12]. A common use of IS architecting is however applied to processes of system and organization integration and interoperability [8, 13]. It has been pointed out that architectural work for integration needs to take place both at the technical and organizational level [14]. In this regard, an analysis of French small and medium sized enterprises showed that the size of the enterprise had great influence of the integration efforts and thus also the resulting technical IT architecture [9].

In terms of scope, IS architectures have mostly been discussed related to single organizations [15]. However, distribution of power, which would also apply to cross-organizational architectures, has been a topic of interest. In this regard, Martin concludes that "In an organization with strong distribution of power, architectural purity can become a secondary concern to organizational acceptability" [16, p. 144]. He reports that this challenge is especially true for federated organizations, which is very relevant for the case of international and regional information systems discussed in this paper.

2.2   Information Infrastructures

A useful concept for capturing the multifaceted nature and roles of architecture is Information Infrastructures (II). II has been defined as "evolving, shared, open, and heterogeneous installed base" [17, p. 60]. Evolving as in enabling change over time, shared by a larger community, open in that there is no clear-cut boundary as to what it includes, heterogeneous in that it consists of socio-technical networks and sub-networks, many of whom are very different in nature, and installed as in always building on something existing. They are pervasive, existing for decades rather than years, and are entangled in yet other IIs beyond their own scope [18].

IIs are never designed from scratch, rather they evolve over time. Architecting from an II perspective is as such not a one-off exercise, but a continuous process of managing evolution. This evolution can be seen as a dialectical process of more autonomous evolution and more directional construction, where the roles of heterogeneity, standards, II builders, politics and institutions must be taken into account [19]. Edwards et al. argues that labels such as designing or building leave us

---

[1] http://www.opengroup.org/togaf/

to think that someone is in control of this process: "Since infrastructures are incremental and modular, they are always constructed in many places (the local), combined and recombined (the modular), and they take on new meaning in both different times and spaces (the contextual) [20].

In light of this, we continue in this paper to look at IS architecture from a processual perspective, where the activity of architecting is seen as managing the evolution of existing practices and systems. Our working definition of architecture is components and the relationships between them, with the components typically being organizational entities, and the relationships signifying the information flows between these entities. As congruent with II theory, we hold that such an architecture is not static, and that it's evolution is not in the power of an "architect". Rather, it is contested and in continuous development. We now proceed with a presentation of the methodology applied, and the empirical material through which we will apply this understanding of architecting.

3   Methods

The research described in this paper has taken place within a large international action research program called the Health Information Systems Program, HISP. HISP has been on-going since the mid-nineties, doing research, development, and implementation of health information systems related activities [22]. In this paper we discuss two implementations HISP has been involved in; strengthening the national HIS in Ghana, and creating a regional HIS for the West African Health Organization (WAHO).

Two of the authors have been actively involved in the practical work described in the paper, related to evaluating, planning, designing, implementing, training for, and continuously supporting, health information systems for management. One of these authors has been involved in the region since 2007, including the early work with WAHO since 2010, while the other author has been heavily engaged in the work in Ghana since 2011, and with WAHO since 2013.

This study spans several sub-projects and several years, for which there has not been defined an overall research design in line with canonical action research principles. However, the practical work in Ghana and with WAHO has followed a cyclical application of planning, implementation, evaluation, and dissemination, which are key characteristics of action research [23, 24, 25]. Planning and evaluation of activities have taken place in cycles of various lengths; in day-to-day work, evaluation has been continuous, while longer evaluation cycles typically have centred around fieldwork and workshops. In the longer term, planning and evaluation have been carried out in relation to yearly events organized by WAHO. The action taking has taken place both in Ghana, WAHO headquarters in Burkina Faso, and various locations throughout the region, and at a distance from the authors home institution. The work at "home" has typically involved database design, evaluation, and re-design, including analysis of all sorts of existing requirements as formalized in indicator lists, data collection forms, and the like. The work in the "field" has included all related activities for health information system strengthening, including technical and organizational. The articulation and dissemination of knowledge has been documented by a range of scientific publications [26, 27], policy opinions [28], and official recommendations to other actors in the field of HIS [29].

One of the authors was primarily involved in the early stages of working with WAHO since 2010, after having worked with similar issues in the region for some years prior to this. His main interaction with WAHO was in participating at early workshops to assess the status of HIS in the region, and advising on the role of WAHO to strengthen HIS across the member countries Included in this was advising how WAHO should develop their own HIS capacity, including a regional data warehouse for public access. As such, the author was mostly involved with policy work, and less with the practical and technical implementation of the data warehouse. However, responsibilities and roles relating to this data warehouse were discussed extensively in Sierra Leone, one of the member states of WAHO. Data was collected from this work through taking notes at the workshops, studying WAHO documents such as vision statements and indicator lists, and email correspondence related to the practical work.

The author involved in the Ghana case has been part of that project since 2011, and has since then spent between five and six months in Ghana. He has been involved mostly with the national HIS unit in Accra, but also with various sub-national offices and facilities in 7 of the 10 regions. The main data collection methods have been field notes, participant observation and unstructured interviews with staff in different positions and at different levels of the health system. When not in the field in Ghana, electronic communication has been maintained on a regular basis - both with the national HIS team, and with end-users throughout Ghana using an electronic messaging system built into the HIS software.

The same author has also been involved with the regional data warehouse project since 2013, participating in a workshop organized by WAHO for HIS representatives from all countries as well as partners in 2013; visiting the WAHO headquarters and the national HIS and disease surveillance teams in Burkina Faso in 2014; and participating in the planning and design of the regional data warehouse. The main data collection methods have been field notes, unstructured interviews, minutes from meetings and participation in the database design.

3.1   Data Analysis

As was discussed above, the three authors have different empirical backgrounds: one has been involved with the WAHO project; one has been involved in Ghana, and later the WAHO project; while one has not been directly involved in any of the two cases. In seminars and ad-hoc meetings between the authors, the empirical material has been presented and discussed, and those elements that were seen as relevant for understanding the architectural process involved identified.

In this work, we have found that the diversity we have in terms of empirical background has been a strength. Two authors have been able to provide rich empirical data and in-depth knowledge of the two cases, while one author has been in an outsider position and as such has been able to ask questions and see relevant points that have not been obvious for the insiders.

The data analysis has focused on describing architectural characteristics of the two implementations, using a loose definition of architecture as components and the relationships between them. As such, drawings were made to identify information flows, where components were typically organizational entities, and the relationships signifying information flows. The main actors influencing the nature of the relationships were then discussed. Architectural characteristics at the software level has not been part of the analysis.

Using our definition of architecture, we have then looked at how the components and their relationships have been negotiated and changed over time. For example, in the case of WAHO described below, the negotiation processes are on-going, and change content as the project advances and tighter integration is achieved. Our analysis would then focus on the reasons for agreeing to, say, having actor A do data collection rather than actor B.

4   Case: Architecting Large Scale HIS in West Africa

This paper analyses on-going work to strengthen health information systems in West Africa. We will present two cases, which, while sharing similar objectives and approaches, differ in organizational structure and hence pose different trajectories of architecting towards these similar objectives. Our aim is not to compare the cases, but using both of them offers a richer perspective on architectures and the processes of architecting involved. The two cases are that of the West African Health Organization (WAHO) and Ghana.

4.1   WAHO

In late 2010, WAHO co-hosted a workshop for interoperable health information systems. The motivation behind this interoperability work, which was also supported by World Health Organization (WHO), was improving their system for regional health monitoring and policymaking. Several countries attending the workshop were using the DHIS 2 software as their national data warehouse for health indicators. Sierra Leone had been working with it since 2007, but also Gambia and Ghana were in the early process of setting it up. Based on this, WAHO suggested that they also would look into DHIS 2, and assessing the potential for it to be used as a regional data warehouse. They initiated collaboration with the HISP network, which was supporting the development and implementation of DHIS 2, and laid out their vision: WAHO serving the region with essential health data from all countries through an online repository, with high quality and frequent updates. WAHO was already working on its own solution for this, but had limited resources to take that solution to the sophistication envisioned. The new online repository would thus replace this, and because the DHIS 2 platform was already widely used in the region, it would also be used for the regional data warehouse.

In the following years, several related activities took place around health information systems strengthening and the development of the regional data warehouse. An assessments of country HIS in the region was done in 2011-12, and based on this a HIS policy document was developed and finally approved at a ministerial meeting in 2013. The policy included guidelines for HIS strengthening across the region, and reaffirmed the vision for a regional data warehouse based in WAHO.

A set of about 80 essential indicators to be included in the regional data warehouse had been developed. These essential indicators covered many different areas, including demographics, disease burden, health service utilization, health financing, human resources and epidemic diseases. For the different types of indicators, expected frequencies of reporting from countries to WAHO were defined, ranging from weekly for the epidemic diseases, to every few years for the demographic indicators. By covering such a diverse set of areas, the list of essential indicators assumes a relatively high level of HIS integration at the national level.

It was decided that the regional data warehouse should hold data aggregated by districts for each country. This was a challenge in a region where there are huge differences in the size and structure of the countries, and consequently in the number and size of the administrative levels. The solution chosen was to define two sub-national administrative levels in the regional data warehouse, and let each country decide which administrative levels in their country corresponded to each of these levels in the regional data warehouse, as shown in figure 1.

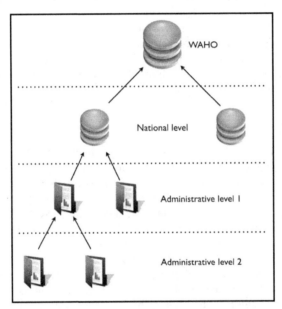

Fig. 1. The organizational hierarchy of the WAHO regional data warehouse. The arrows illustrate the flow of information, first from the sub-national level to a national database, and from the national database to the regional data warehouse.

It was decided to have a pilot phase including five of the fifteen countries. Of the five countries selected, four used the DHIS 2 software and was thus already working closely with HISP, something that was seen as an advantage. Discussions with the pilot countries revealed large variations in what data was available in each country, at what frequency it was collected, whether it was available in a central HIS database or in separate data "silos" run by the area-specific programs, and the format in which the data was stored.

HISP was given the task of developing mechanisms of transferring metadata and data from countries to WAHO. Because 12 of the 15 countries in the region are now using DHIS 2 in some way, or have plans to do so, the focus was on developing reporting procedures for these countries first. Developing routines for the other countries would require in-country work to understand their systems. The transfer mechanism and procedure that was developed and proposed had to take several issues into account:

- To ensure timeliness of reporting from countries to WAHO, an automated transfer mechanism that did not require any action on the part of WAHO or the countries would be preferable.
- To simplify maintenance of the data transfer mechanism, as much of the logic and computer code as possible should be running on WAHO's server rather than in the countries.
- Countries should be able to verify the data before it could be used or published by WAHO.
- Countries should be in control of what data WAHO has access to, and be able to revoke this access at any time.

Based on this, a solution for the countries using DHIS 2 was proposed in which WAHO is given access to read the essential indicator data directly in the country databases, and to transfer it to the regional data warehouse. However, the data will not be published until the countries have verified and approved that the data is correct through an approval mechanism built into the data warehouse. Furthermore, countries can at any time revoke WAHO's access to their system simply by disabling their user account, and countries thus remain in control over their own data.

A challenge with the regional data warehouse was financing the work required, both to establish the data warehouse in WAHO and to set up the required reporting structure in the countries. In late 2013, representatives from the World Bank were introduced to the project, and they suggested that some of the project could be financed as part of a three-year West African Regional Disease Surveillance Capacity Strengthening (WARDS) project, which was starting in 2014. To increase the relevance of the regional data warehouse in relation to the WARDS project, WAHO together with HISP decided to adjust the roadmap: instead of starting with the full list of indicators for some pilot countries, it was decided to start with a focus on the disease surveillance indicators for all countries.

There is already a structure in place for weekly reporting of data on epidemic diseases from countries to WAHO, however, there are several problems with this reporting. Firstly, reporting from countries is intermittent and often delayed. Only about half of the 15 countries sent all reports to WAHO in 2013, and some countries only sent a handful of reports. Secondly, countries send data in different formats and with different levels of granularity. While some countries send WHO-developed excel templates with district level data, the majority sends bulletins in PDF or Microsoft Word formats with only national-level data.

Another complicating factor is that the programs in charge of epidemic diseases are seldom integrated with the national HIS. This means that for the regional data warehouse to receive data on epidemic diseases, there will either have to be developed a data transfer mechanism directly from the disease control program to WAHO, or the data on epidemic diseases must be integrated with the HIS on the national level. Ghana is a typical example of a country where data collection on epidemic diseases is not integrated with the HIS: while weekly data on epidemic diseases is in fact included in the DHIS 2-based HIS, the disease control program responsible for reporting to WAHO is using their own parallel reporting system.

4.2   Ghana

By the time of the before-mentioned WAHO workshop in late 2010, Ghana had just decided to adopt DHIS 2 as their national HIS, simultaneously pushing for integration of the data collected by the area-specific health programs such as Malaria, HIV/AIDS and Immunization with the national HIS. The implementation was lead by the Policy, Planning, Monitoring and Evaluation (PPME) division of the Ghana Health Service (GHS), the implementing agency of the Ministry of Health. PPME worked to bring all the programs on board with the idea of an integrated national information system, and somewhat reluctantly virtually all programs agreed - though most retained their parallel reporting systems while waiting to see whether the integrated data warehouse would succeed.

A similar effort had been made a few years earlier, when a custom-designed system based on Microsoft Access was installed in all regional- and district offices, and in the government hospitals throughout the country. This system had incorporated data for some of the area-specific programs and divisions, but had for several reasons come to be regarded as a failure. The software development had been done with funding from the European Union, and when the project ended there were no resources to continue maintaining and improving the software. This problem was amplified by the fact that the software itself was quite inflexible and required changes in the source code even for minor changes in data sets or reports. The programs did not see the system as being able to meet their reporting needs, and therefore reverted to using parallel data collection systems. In addition to this, it proved technically challenging to keep the metadata in hundreds of standalone databases compatible with each other over time, something that was required for merging of the district databases into a regional database, and the regional databases into a national database.

DHIS 2 was seen as a platform that could solve many of the problems of the previous system. It was Free and Open Source Software (FOSS) that was already in use in many countries, thus there was no cost related to software development or maintenance. This was especially important since there was no funding for the implementation outside the regular budgets. Furthermore, DHIS 2 could be configured and maintained through the user interface, without changes to the source code being required. Finally, by virtue of being Web-based, it could be deployed nationally on a single server and accessed by users over the Internet, thus avoiding the problem of standalone databases becoming "out of synch" with each other.

Because the routines, experience and much of the infrastructure were already in place across the country from the previous system, the implementation of DHIS 2 was largely seen by the Ghana Health Service as a "software update" rather than an implementation of a new, complex information system. A small team of administrators in the PPME division was given the task of configuring the system for the Ghanian context, with support from HISP in the form of assistance from one of the authors. While PPME was in charge of deploying the information system and training end-users, it was up to the different health programs and divisions to define and decide on the data sets to be included in the system. They generally used the same data sets that they had already been using, carrying over the existing overlaps and duplications in the data being collected at the facility level.

While the implementation of DHIS 2 was seen as a "software update" by the implementers, the move from an offline, distributed system to one that was centralized and accessed over the Internet was a big change in many ways. One important difference was the need for Internet connectivity to use the system. Due largely to the rapidly improving mobile network coverage in recent years, which allowed users to connect to the Internet using modems, this was not a major problem except in a few of the most remote locations. It is important to note that only the largest health facilities are computerized and use the system directly, the majority instead send their reports on paper to the district office where it is entered into DHIS 2. Another change was the sudden need for skills in server management and maintenance for the one central server. These skills where not available in the PPME division, and HISP has thus ended up providing assistance in server administration for an extended period of time.

The move to an online system also led to changes in the roles and responsibilities for the officers working at lower levels. The flow of information was still meant to follow the organisational hierarchy from the facility, through sub-district-, district- and regional level (see Figure 2), with each level being in charge of ensuring the quality and validity of the data. While the information had previously followed the same hierarchy, as paper reports, on USB-stick or in emails, the new centralised system means that all data is stored in the national database directly, from the point of entry at the facility or district level. Especially the regions, but also to some extent the districts, were thus no longer part of the actual information flow, though they could still access the information and were still responsible for its validity.

The system was opened for users in April 2012, after a training phase of several months where approximately one thousand users were trained. Because there were limited funds available for the implementation, different partners and donors sponsored training of different regions. Since the national rollout, some of the area-specific health programs and divisions have shown increasing interest in the system. The Malaria program, for example, has now ended their parallel reporting, relying on the integrated HIS for their data needs.

DHIS 2 in Ghana was meant to be not only the backbone of the HIS for collection, storage and analysis of information, but also a data warehouse that would be interoperable with and receive aggregate data from other systems, for example electronic patient records systems and human resource systems. However, after nearly two years, no integration with other systems has materialized. An important reason for this appears to be the lack of stable third-party systems in use to interoperate with. Both from within GHS and from HISP group at the University of Oslo, it has been suggested that the patient-based module of DHIS 2 could take over for some of the systems that were still in early phases of development. This led to some complaints among the different actors in the health sector that DHIS 2 was replacing other systems rather than interoperating with them. At the same time, several of the health programs that were initially developing their own systems, such as the Tuberculosis and Immunization programs, are now in fact planning to pilot the patient-based module of DHIS 2 as an alternative to developing new systems from scratch.

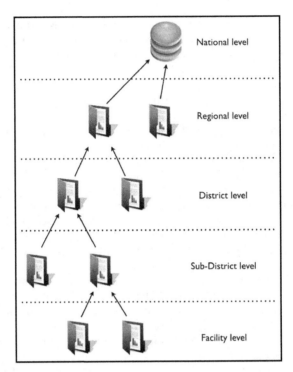

Fig. 2. The organizational hierarchy of the Ghana health information system. The arrows illustrate the flow of information from the facility level, through the three sub-national levels, to the national database.

5   Discussion

Taking as a point of departure our definition of architecture as the components and the relation between them, we argue that while the architectural drawing or blueprints of the Ghana and WAHO information infrastructures (Figure 1 and 2 above) are very similar, in reality they contain very different processes and division of labour, which are reconfigured at irregular intervals. As such, we find that a view of architectures as a drawing or blueprint is inadequate [7, 10]. In this section we discuss the two cases and their peculiarities, and how they may inform our understanding of architectures. We take a view of information systems as information infrastructures, acknowledging their complexities, social and technical aspects, historicity, and evolutionary development.

A main difference between WAHO and Ghana is the organizational spectrum covered. In the case of WAHO, there is a "horizontal division" between the regional body and the various countries, where the countries have autonomy and a veto concerning their own data. In other words, it resembles a federated organizational structure. Our findings resonate with Martin [16] in that "architectural principles" may take second importance after organizational agreement in such cases. For instance, a meta-data regime assuring coherence throughout the WAHO database and the respective country databases will not be easy in this case. Meta-data integrity throughout this extended II will not be enforced as it may jeopardize the organizational agreement.

On the other side, many countries in the region have "vertical divisions" between the various health programs at national level, for example Ghana where the IDSR unit dealing with epidemic diseases is independent of PPME, which is in charge of the HIS. This means that parallel reporting structures may co-exist, as long as the various health programs are not enforced or convinced to use the national data warehouse. Even the programs that are integrated in the national data warehouse are themselves defining what data to be collected within their program areas.

With the regional data warehouse, WAHO is attempting to work across both the horizontal and the vertical divisions. The horizontal division by asking countries to let WAHO access their data, and the vertical division by asking countries to make available all data for the essential indicators in one data repository – essentially requesting that an integrated HIS is created at the national level. Failing to do so, something that is not unlikely in at least some of the 15 countries, will result in a different and far more complex structure from that of Figure 1, with several parallel flows of data, and potentially multiple sets of organisational hierarchies for the sub-national levels in some of the countries. Obscured from the architectural drawing of Figure 1 is thus not only the negotiations and politics involved in reporting of data from the national level to WAHO, but also the internal politics within countries on the establishment of national data warehouses.

For the WAHO database, it was decided that the organization would itself collect data from the various countries. This is a clear example of division of labour, which may reflect the relative importance seen by WAHO to get hold of the data. In Ghana, the data-collecting levels will themselves access the online database to enter their data, which is a mirror image of the division of labour between WAHO and Ghana at the national level.

The WAHO system was set up to collect a wide range of different data, from demographics to key health program data. However, in order to attract the support of a large international partner to fund the project, WAHO opted for scaling down from the essential indicator list, which had been agreed upon, to a subset of data dealing with epidemic diseases (IDSR) for the initial period. This leads to changes not only in the information being reported, but also in what unit WAHO will be working with at the national level. As discussed above, the IDSR data might not easily be found in the countries, at least not in the "preferred" source of the national DHIS 2-implementation. While work on country reporting to WAHO had already begun on the essential indicators, a new set of actors is now suddenly playing the lead role at the national level.

In the case of Ghana, the influences of external actors on the architectural process are less clear-cut. For example, HISP has proposed the use of the patient-based module of the DHIS software on several occasions, but it is not clear if this has been a significant factor in recent decisions to migrate several standalone systems into DHIS contrary to the initial plans. Nonetheless, it demonstrates how different actors influence architectures in ways that are not visible from a blueprint.

The two cases also illustrate how architectures are not static blueprints, but evolve over time. The WAHO database was initially meant to cover all essential indicators from day one, but due to outside influences will now initially focus on only a subset of these indicators. Similarly, the HIS in Ghana has evolved substantially over time, though the overall architecture as presented in Figure 2 has remained the same. It was meant to be an integrated data warehouse for the whole health sector in Ghana, but for a long time was only one of several parallel systems. This has now started to change again. Furthermore, while DHIS 2 in Ghana was envisaged to be a data warehouse that would receive data from other interoperable systems, it is now instead being piloted as an alternative to replace several of those systems

5.1   Architecture as Process of Assigning Roles

In light of the cases of WAHO and Ghana, we propose to see architecture as primarily concerning division of labour, or negotiating roles relating to who will do what, when, and where. More importantly, architecture should not be seen as a drawing, of an ideal vision or current state, but as constantly emerging out of the *architecting* process. This process should be seen as political and contested, meaning that architectural principles, such as modularization and loose coupling, are not necessarily deemed most important.

The management of roles does not only apply to organizations or individuals, but to routines or technology such as DHIS 2. The discussion in Ghana as to what role DHIS 2 should have is illustrative of this. Since there is a functional overlap between several applications, what should decide which one to use? To reduce complexity, it would make sense to use as few applications as possible, but in Ghana the idea of one large system taking over too many roles has also caused concerns. The organizational "harmony" was kept at the expense of reducing amount of applications in use. Power and control over the various systems is also a potential factor in this regards, influencing process of architecting the information infrastructure.

6   Conclusion

IS architecture is not about the "perfect" drawing, using the "perfect" standards. It is much more complex and hence ad-hoc and pragmatic. A key feature of an architecture is the division of labour, or the assignment of roles, which is contested and dynamic. In line with literature on information infrastructures, the negotiation of these roles between various actors leads us to see architectural work more as evolving than being designed and controlled [20]. IS architectures are thus not made on the drawing board, but enacted through organizational behaviour and contestation [10].

Our two cases illustrate this. While the figures presenting the "architectures" for Ghana and WAHO in this paper look similar, the processes and division of labour hidden in these is what makes them disparate. In WAHO, the countries are autonomous, and the system must thus be designed so that countries remain in control of their data. Conversely, in Ghana, the vertical health programs are autonomous, and the system must be adapted to their requirements. The figures also conceal the importance of negotiations between the different actors, including ones that are not part of the architectural drawing. When an opportunity to obtain external funding for the WAHO project arose, this led to direct changes in what information was to be reported from the countries. Finally, we argue that architectures should be seen as processes that evolve over time. WAHO changed their reporting well into the implementation process, substantially changing the content of the information to be reported, and as a consequence also which entity would be responsible for the reporting at the national level. In Ghana, the overall HIS architecture has remained constant, but both the actual information flow and the role of the various organisational levels have changed substantially over time. This is not visible unless one sees architecture as a dynamic process.

For practitioners such as HISP, such a view of architecture should lead to spending more efforts in understanding the various relations at stake. While a blueprint of a perfect situation is a common actor in planning and policy documents, the real architecture lies behind the figure, in the division of labor of the various components. Future research in the described projects will look at strategies of managing such roles.

References

1. Weisz, G.: The Emergence of Medical Specialization in the Nineteenth Century. Bulletin of the History of Medicine 77(3), 536–574 (2003)
2. Norris, A.C.: Current trends and challenges in health informatics. Health Informatics Journal 8(4), 205–213 (2002)
3. Chan, M.: Report by the Director-General to the Executive Board at its 130th Session. World Health Organization (2012)
4. Health Metrics Network. Framework and standards for Country Health Information Systems. World Health Organization (2008)
5. WHO, Systems thinking for health systems strengthening. World Health Organization (2009)
6. Braa, J., Sahay, S.: Integrated Health Information Architecture: Power to the Users. Matrix Publishers, New Delhi (2012)
7. Vassilakopoulou, P., Grisot, M.: Exploring the concept of architecture in Technology and Organization studies. IRIS 36 (2013)
8. Hjort-Madsen, K.: Enterprise architecture implementation and management: A case study on interoperability. In: HICSS 2006 (2006)
9. Bidan, M., Rowe, F., Truex, D.: An empirical study of IS architectures in French SMEs: integration approaches. European Journal of Information Systems 21(3) (2012)
10. Bygstad, B., Pedersen, N.: Arkitektur handler om praktisk arbeid i organisasjonen, ikke en tegning. En forskningsagenda om IT-arkitekters utfordringer, Norsk konferanse for organisasjoners bruk av informasjonsteknologi, NOKOBIT 2012 (2012)
11. Scheil Corneliussen, M.: IT Architecturing–Reconceptualizing Current Notions of Architecture in IS Research. In: ECIS 2008 Proceedings. Paper 154 (2008), http://aisel.aisnet.org/ecis2008/154
12. Buck, S., Ernst, A., Matthes, F., Ramacher, R., Schweda, C.: Using Enterprise Architecture Management Patterns to Complement TOGAF. In: IEEE International Enterprise Distributed Object Computing Conference, EDOC 2009 (2009)
13. Chen, D., Doumeingts, G., Vernadat, F.: Architectures for enterprise integration and interoperability: Past, present and future. Computers in Industry 59(7), 647–659 (2008)

14. Andersson, M., Lindgren, R., Henfridsson, O.: Architectural knowledge in inter-organizational IT innovation. The Journal of Strategic Information Systems 17(1), 19–38 (2008)
15. Hanseth, O., Bygstad, B.: ICT Architecture And Project Risk In Inter-Organizational Settings. In: ECIS 2012 Proceedings, Paper 130 (2012)
16. Martin, A.: Enterprise IT Architecture in Large Federated Organizations: The Art of the Possible. Information Systems Management 29(2), 137–147 (2012)
17. Hanseth, O.: The Economics of Standards. From control to drift: The dynamics of corporate information infrastructures. C. Ciborra. Oxford University Press, Oxford (2000)
18. Monteiro, E., Pollock, N., Hanseth, O., Williams, R.: From Artefacts to Infrastructures. In: Computer Supported Cooperative Work (CSCW), pp. 1–33 (2012)
19. Nielsen, P.: A Conceptual Framework of Information Infrastructure Building, A Case study of the Development of a Content Service Platform for Mobile Phones in Norway. PhD Thesis, University of Oslo (2006)
20. Edwards, M., Hulme, D.: Making a difference: NGOs and Development in a Changing World. Earthscan, London (1992)
21. Braa, J., Hedberg, C.: The Struggle for District-Based Health Information Systems in South Africa. The Information Society (18), 113–127 (2002)
22. Braa, J., Monteiro, E., Sahay, S.: Networks of Action: Sustainable Health Information Systems Across Developing Countries. MIS Quarterly 28(3), 337–362 (2004)
23. Susman, G., Evered, R.: An Assessment of the Scientific Merits of Action Research. Administrative Science Quarterly 23(4), 582–603 (1978)
24. Baskerville, R.L.: Distinguishing action research from participative case studies. Journal of Systems and Information Technology 1(1), 24–43 (1997)
25. Checkland, P., Holwell, S.: Action Research: Its Nature and Validity. Systemic Practice and Action Research 11(1), 9–21 (1998)
26. Sæbø, J., Braa, J., Kossi, E.K., Jalloh, M., Manya, A.: Developing decentralised health information systems in developing countries –cases from Sierra Leone and Kenya. Journal of Community Informatics 9(2) (2013)
27. Sæbø, J.I., Kossi, E.K., Titlestad, O.H., Tohouri, R.R., Braa, J.: Comparing strategies to integrate health information systems following a data warehouse approach in four countries. Information Technology for Development 17(1), 42–60 (2011)
28. Braa, J.: A data warehouse approach can manage multiple data sets. Bulletin of the World Health Organization 83, 638–639 (2005)
29. Braa, J., Sahay, S., Kossi, E.K., Mbondji, P.: ECOWAS Health Information Systems Policy and Strategy Document: West African Health Organization 56 (2012)

The Impact of Enterprise Crowdsourcing
on Company Innovation Culture:
The Case of an Engineering Consultancy

Ada Scupola[1] and Hanne Westh Nicolajsen[2]

[1] Roskilde University, Building 44.3, DK-4000 Roskilde, Denmark
[2] Department for Communication, Aalborg University CPH
2450 Copenhagen SV, Denmark
ada@ruc.dk, westh@hum.aau.dk

Abstract. In this article we investigate how enterprise crowdsourcing can be used to change the innovation culture in a consultancy company by conducting an empirical investigation in a large engineering consultancy. The analysis shows that enterprise crowdsourcing has created a new and different awareness of innovation, empowered the employees, supported collaboration across different organizational units to a new extent thus contributing to small changes in the innovation culture of the organization.

Keywords: Organizational culture, innovation culture, crowdsourcing, social media.

1   Introduction

Crowdsourcing draw on the collective intelligence of the crowd to collect new ideas for innovation purposes [1, 2]. Most of the literature investigating crowdsourcing focuses mainly on populations that are external to an organization, and often take a business to consumer approach [3, 4, 5]. However crowdsourcing systems trying to harness the knowledge of the employees within an organization boundary are lately flourishing. Following Vukovic [6], we refer to these systems as enterprise crowdsourcing systems. One of the few studies focusing on enterprise crowdsourcing was conducted by Bjelland and Wood (2008) showing how IBM leverages its firm-wide intelligence located at geographically dispersed sites through a process called "innovation jams". Previous literature has also investigated the relationship between culture and information and communication technology in different contexts [8,9,10, 11]. However, only a few studies have dealt with the impact of IT on culture in an organizational context [8]. Therefore we investigate the following research question: How might the use of an enterprise crowdsourcing system influence the innovation culture in an engineering consulting company?

To answer the research question we conduct a case study of an enterprise crowdsourcing platform called "Idébørsen," which was used to help generate innovation ideas from employees and by so doing influenced the innovation culture of the organization.

T.H. Commisso et al. (Eds.): SCIS 2014, LNBIP 186, pp. 105–120, 2014.

The remainder of this paper is structured as follows. The next section reviews the literature on organizational culture as well as the emerging work on enterprise crowdsourcing. The next section describes the research methods used to gather the data. A rich description of the case study organization and crowdsourcing platform is then provided, which is followed by the results, a discussion and conclusions.

2   Theoretical Grounding

There is a growing debate in the organizational culture literature as to whether culture can be consciously and objectively managed. Pliskin et al. [11] states that the organizational culture literature can be divided into two streams. The first one is descriptive and has the purpose of understanding and describing organizational culture. The second one, which has a normative approach, assumes that organizational culture can be managed and controlled. Within this stream of literature a few studies have focused on the role of new technologies in managing organizational culture [9, 10]. In this section we first present and discuss the concept of corporate culture, especially focusing on the few studies that specifically have looked at the role of IT in influencing corporate culture. Based on these studies we build an analytical framework consisting of a number of cultural dimensions derived from previous literature. This framework will be used to investigate, identify and analyze along which dimensions cultural changes have taken place in the company investigated in this study as a consequence of the crowdsourcing process.

2.1   Organizational Culture

Previous studies have investigated different aspects of culture at the national (e.g. Hofstede, 1997), organizational [13] and subunit levels [14]. Culture is often described in terms of the assumptions, values and artifacts or practices that exist within an organization [13]. Following prior research, we examine innovation culture in terms of the core set of attitudes and practices shared by members of the firm in relation to the innovation task [15]. According to Tellis et al. [15], "scholars of corporate culture have called for middle-range descriptions of corporate culture – descriptions that preserve the holistic aspects of the construct while acknowledging the particulars of the tasks or outcomes being studied". This has, for example, been the approach used in the examination of the role of corporate culture in employee promotion and dismissal outcomes by [12]. Literature on organizational culture [16, 17, 18] has developed models and tools based on several dimensions to operationalize and measure the effect of culture. Denison [16] developed a model asserting that organizational culture can be described by four general dimensions, each of which can be further described by some sub-dimensions: 1) Mission - Strategic Direction and Intent, Goals and Objectives and Vision; 2) Adaptability - Creating Change, Customer Focus and Organizational Learning; 3) Involvement - Empowerment, Team Orientation and Capability Development; 4) Consistency - Core Values, Agreement, Coordination/Integration. Denison's model also allows culture to be described broadly as externally or internally focused as well as flexible versus stable. The model has been typically used to diagnose cultural problems in organizations. Inspired by previous literature we refer to innovation culture as the artifacts and practices that within an organization have to do with the innovation activity and can eventually be influenced by information and communication technologies (ICTs). Therefore, based on prior research [15, 11, 9, 10] we identify a number of dimensions of organizational culture such as empowerment, customer service, team working etc. that are summarized in Table 1 and that are used as the starting point to investigate innovation culture in this paper.

2.2   IT and Culture

A number of studies [11] suggest that there is a potential to use IT for managing and stimulating cultural change and some authors have developed strategies or guidelines on how to conduct such a process [19]. On the other hand as pointed out by Doherty and Doig [9] there is also a body of studies that believe that organizational culture is difficult to change even over relatively long periods. This is the case especially when the assumptions about the organizational culture of an IT system are in contrast with the actual culture of the organization deploying it [20].

Leidner and Kayworth [8] in an extensive literature review of the relationship between culture and information technology identified six main themes under which this literature can be grouped. Their analysis included three levels of organizational culture: national, organizational and subunit. However, given our research interest, we only focus here on the organizational culture level. The first theme "Culture and Information Systems Development (ISD)" includes only three studies at the organizational level of analysis and they are all concerned with the question of how culture influences information systems design. The second theme "Culture and Information Technology Adoption and Diffusion" identifies studies dealing with culture's influence on IT adoption and diffusion at the organizational level. Leidner and Kayworth [8] conclude that value orientations (national, organizational, or subculture) may predispose certain social groups toward either favorable or unfavorable IT adoption and diffusion behaviors. The third theme "Culture, Information Technology Use and Outcomes" includes studies dealing with the particular cultural values related to user satisfaction and successful implementation of IS at the organizational level. The main conclusion that Leidner and Kayworth [8] draw from these studies is that the notion of fit figures prominently in this stream of research. The fourth theme "Culture, IT Management, and Strategy" addresses the relationship between cultural values and IT strategies. Leidner and Kayworth [8] conclude that "there is very little research devoted to examining the role of national or organizational culture in the process of IT planning, in achieving IT alignment, or in the result of IT planning (the actual IT strategy)" (p. 370). The fifth theme deals with "The Impact of IT on Culture" and is therefore the most relevant to our study. We further discuss the findings from this theme below. Finally, the sixth theme "IT Culture" focuses on the very notion of an IT culture defined by Leidner and Kayworth [8] as the values attributed to IT by a group and is based on the assumption that organizational stakeholders attribute certain values to information technology.

Table 1. Dimensions of Organizational Culture

Dimension	Explanation	Literature
Customer Service	The degree to which an organization collectively adopts an external customer orientation, as opposed to an internal process orientation.	(Cooper, 1994; Hofstede, 1997:191)
Flexibility	The extent to which an organization is predisposed to adaptation in the response to changing circumstances in preference to favoring stability and settled order, whenever possible.	(Cooper, 1994; Major, 2002)
Empowerment	The degree to which decision-making is delegated to individual employees, in preference to centralizing it within a group of key managers.	(Pliskin et al, 1993; Morgan, 1998: 144)
Innovation and Action Orientation	The urgency of taking actions and the importance of encouraging innovation and rapid response to changes in the environment.	(Pliskin et al, 1993)
Risk taking	The importance of taking risky decisions as e.g. investment in new ventures or purchase of manufacturing equipment	(Pliskin et al, 1993)
Integration and Lateral Interdependence	The importance of cooperation (instead of competition) and communication among organizational subunits in order to achieve overall organizational goals. This is reflected in the amount of encouragement given to sharing information and to mutual understanding of difficulties.	(Pliskin et al, 1993)
Autonomy in Decision making	The importance of delegating responsibility for important decisions.	(Pliskin et al, 1993)
Performance Orientation	The nature of demands that are placed upon organization members in relation to their expected performance and its accountability and appraisal.	(Pliskin et al, 1993)
Top Management Contact	The nature of manager-subordinate relations.	(Pliskin et al, 1993)
Reward Orientation	The nature of the reward structure e.g. if compensation should be related to performance	(Pliskin et al, 1993)
Team-working	Encouragement of team spirit	(Doherty and Perry, 2001)

Only two studies were identified under the fifth theme of "The Impact of IT on Culture" within the organizational context. The study by Doherty and Doig [9] examined the influence of improved data warehousing capabilities on the organizational culture. They found that improved data warehousing capabilities were an essential catalyst in transforming espoused cultural values into reality and that change had taken place with respect to the cultural dimensions of customer service, flexibility, empowerment, and integration. In another study, Doherty and Perry [10] examined the influence of a new workflow management system (WMS) on organizational culture. Their results show that the implementation of the WMS strengthened organizational culture values related to customer orientation, flexibility, quality focus, and performance orientation. Finally [20], even though not explicitly talking about organizational culture argues that for radical organizational changes to take place there is a need for what she defines as techno-change, which is change processes where IT solutions and organizational elements are mutually aligned to create sustaining change. During this process, [20] argues that the organization culture may be affected; however it is not IT per see but rather the organizational setup which creates these changes.

2.3   Enterprise Crowdsourcing

The term crowdsourcing, derived in part from Surowiecki's [21] notion of the "wisdom of crowds," refers to an emerging set of approaches taking advantage of a large number of distributed users (mainly online) to solve problems, perform micro tasks, provide ideas, thus leveraging the superiority of large aggregations of people over individuals [22, 23,24, 2]. However some definitions [6, 25] point out to the use of crowdsourcing systems as a new on-line distributed problem solving and production model in which networked people collaborate to complete a task [25]. Advantages of this approach include relieving concerns with appropriability of the ideas generated [26]. Crowdsourcing systems draw on the collective intelligence of the crowd to collect new ideas for innovation purposes [1, 2]. Most of the literature investigating crowdsourcing focuses mainly on populations that are external to an organization [e.g. 3, 4, 5], even though many platform support idea collection both external and internal to an organization. One well known crowdsourcing platform is Innocentive, which is also the name of the company hosting it. Innocentive accepts by commission research and development problems in a broad range of domains such as engineering, computer science, math, chemistry, life sciences and frames them as "challenge problems" for anyone to solve. The company gives cash awards ranging between 10,000 and 100,000 dollars for the best solutions to solvers who meet the challenge criteria [5]. Another well-known software platform, targeting organization employees is IBM's "innovation jam". Bjelland and Wood [7] show how IBM leveraged its firm-wide intelligence located at geographically dispersed sites through a process called "innovation jams". Finally Andriole [23] in a comprehensive study of the business impact of Web 2.0 technologies found that Web 2.0 technologies for internal applications "have little impact on the innovation process. There are spotty innovation applications of crowdsourcing for R&D and selected applications of folksonomies, RSS filters, and mashups, but the area is generally not affected (p. 69)". For external applications, Andriole [23] found instead that "Web 2.0 tools, techniques, and especially attitudes will alter the innovation process in many industries by facilitating direct communication and collaboration among creators and buyers of new products and services (p.69)".

Table 2. Definitions of crowdsourcing (Adapted from Vucovic et al., 2009)

	Definition: Crowdsourcing is...
Alonso and Lease	... The outsourcing of tasks to a large group of people instead of assigning such tasks to an in-house employee or contractor.
Bederson and Quinn	... People being paid to do web-based tasks posted by requestors.
Brabham	... An online, distributed problem solving and production model already in use by for profit organizations such as Threadless, iStock...
Brabham	... A strategic model to attract an interested, motivated crowd of individuals capable of providing solutions superior in quality and quantity to those that even traditional forms of business can.
Buecheler et al.	... A special case of such collective intelligence.
Burger-Helmchen and Penin	... One way for a firm to access external knowledge.
Chanal and Caron-	... The opening of the innovation process of a firm to integrate numerous and
Vucovic	... New on-line distributed problem solving and production model in which networked people collaborate to complete a task.
Vucovic et al.	... A new online distributed production model in which people collaborate and may be awarded to complete task.

On the basis of this introduction to the literature on organizational culture, IT and culture, and enterprise crowdsourcing, there appear to be good reasons to expect that enterprise crowdsourcing can influence the innovation culture of an organization. By definition, it enables a much larger population of employees to play a role in the generation of ideas - influencing many of the organization culture dimensions listed in Table 1. It can enhance an organization's flexibility, empowerment, the innovation and action orientation, and integration and lateral interdependence (see Table 1). In addition, to the extent that good ideas generated in an enterprise crowdsourcing system are rewarded, we might imagine a change in the organization's reward orientation. We can also speculate that, since a crowdsourcing system has the potential to make the contributions of employees more visible, the spirit of collaboration or team work might be encouraged. Overall, based on our brief literature review, we propose that enterprise crowdsourcing can be purposefully used to change the innovation culture of an organization.

3   Research Method

A case study of a Danish engineering consultancy (from now on The Company) was conducted to understand how enterprise crowdsourcing can influence the innovation culture of an organization. A case study is considered an appropriate research method to investigate real-life contexts, such as the use of enterprise crowdsourcing where control over the context is not possible [27]. Inspired by Yin [27] Table 3 summarizes the steps taken to ensure reliability and validity during the study.

The main data collection method was semi-structured interviews with open-ended questions. The interviewees included key relevant employees, project managers and directors dealing with innovation and crowdsourcing at The Company as well as the crowdsourcing platform provider (See Table 4 for details about the interviews). Moreover, an ongoing dialogue with the company has taken place in order to identify any misunderstandings and to obtain additional insights both by telephone and per e-mail. The themes of the interviews, besides background information about the respondents, were based on how the crowdsourcing process had impacted the several dimensions of organizational culture identified in Table 1.

Table 3. Reliability and validity of data

Reliability Through		Validity Through
Case study protocol Informant profiles and contact information Representative list of interview questions List of other potential themes to be explored in the interview	Case study database Recorded audiotapes Interview transcripts of each unit Transcripts of e-mail and telephonic discussions with informants Company documents relating to the mixed crowdsourcing process, websites, access to Idebørsen	Multiple sources of evidence Interview transcripts; telephone and e-mail discussions; Idebørsen software platform access; information available on the web sites of The Company and the social media service provider; documents provided by The Company Establishing chain of evidence In the case description, we have cited extensively from the contents of the case study database. "The circumstances of each data collection activity" was carefully recorded, and the data collection closely followed the case study protocol (Kirsch 2004). Thus the chain of evidence presented helps link the empirical material with the findings Review of case drafts and article The initial draft of the case was reviewed by The Company

Documentation review and field notes were complementary data collection methods. Sources include corporate websites and brochures about the crowdsourcing process, and other internal documents such as schemes to submit an idea, samples of submitted ideas, the winning ideas, criteria for idea selection and news media. The researchers also gained access to the crowdsourcing platform for a period of time. The latter gave us a sense of how the social medium was functioning.

Table 4. Data on Interviews

Number of interviews	24
From HQ	14
From Regional offices	8 (4 regional Offices)
Other	1 customer 1 supplier
Duration of interviews	Normal 1-1.5 h (15) Short ca. 30 min (9)
Positions of informants	Competence Manager Innovation Director Innovation Champion Project Manager Project Member Idebørsen team members Marketing Director

In our case study we use so-called rich descriptions [28] by combining interviews with other secondary material. The data were analyzed by looking for the cultural dimensions that were affected by the introduction of Idébørsen in The Company. When analyzing the data, one challenge has been that sometimes the respondent statements could fit under several dimensions.

3.1 The Case Company and Its Challenges with Innovation Culture

The Company is a part of a global engineering, design and consultancy group, headquartered and founded in Denmark. Overall, the group employs about 10,000 experts worldwide and has a strong presence in Northern Europe, Russia, India and the Middle East. The Danish part of Company counts 1600 employees. In The Company, innovation has traditionally occurred and developed in the context of consulting projects. However, over the last few years The Company has shifted focus on innovation that is not only linked to specific consulting projects, but might be of more general applicability and interest throughout the company. Therefore, over the past few years The Company has established a number of initiatives to increase innovation awareness among employees, change the innovation culture, and help their employees "think out of the box". The company firmly believes that the employees possess valuable knowledge that could be a source of innovative ideas and hope to turn the most promising ideas into practice. Since 2007 two main initiatives aimed at strengthening innovation and the innovation culture outside the scope of specific projects has been undertaken in The Company. The first initiative, called the "Innovation bank", was a paper-based competition internal to the company supporting interesting ideas from employees that had significant revenue potential. The second, which is a further development of the Innovation Bank, is Idébørsen, an enterprise crowdsourcing system to collect ideas from employees and company partners. Idebørsen is the focus of this paper.

Idébørsen is a software platform for the generation and management of ideas from employees and external partners. The software includes a number of features that enhance interaction and collaboration including voting and commenting on others' ideas. Idebørsen is similar to the Groupsystem tools developed at the Center for The

Management of Information at the University of Arizona (http://www.cmi.arizona.edu/research/collaboration). In fact both Idebørsen and the collaboration tools developed at University of Arizona provide users with the power and flexibility to help groups perform complex tasks such as brainstorming, list building, information gathering, voting, organizing, prioritizing, and consensus building. Each employee is given an amount of virtual money at the beginning of the crowdsourcing experiment, which they can invest into the ideas contributed by others. At any point in time, the spot value of an idea –together with the comments that support it– is proxied by the aggregate investment positions held on it relative to all other ideas. The software platform automatically ranks the ideas according to their spot value. The higher the spot value at any given point in time, the higher the ranking of the idea.

3.2   The Crowdsourcing Process

In line with the technical characteristics of the software platform, the crowdsourcing process had the main aim of online organizational brainstorming. At the beginning of the crowdsourcing process, a few strategic themes had been formulated by top management as a frame for brainstorming. This crowdsourcing process has been run twice over two years at The Company. Both times the idea collection process lasted six weeks. After the idea posting and trading period expired, prizes were given to the ideas with the highest spot value in each theme, a prize to the best trader and a prize to the best commentator. These prizes were symbolic such as an IPad. The highest ranked idea within each different theme was also directly entered into a pool of ideas to be considered for further development and implementation. In addition, the rest of the ideas (approx. 100) were screened by the innovation team to select 20 ideas for further consideration. This screening process was based on a number of criteria developed by the innovation team in charge of Idebørsen. The criteria were clear and transparent to all participants. The 20 selected ideas were then presented to the management group and 5 of these ideas were selected for further development together with the 5 highest ranked ideas in Idébørsen. A number of work hours were then allocated to the idea owner and several experts (1-2) were assigned to further develop each idea and define the implementation needs. The crowdsourcing project culminated with an innovation day, where the three winning ideas were selected for final implementation. This day included speeches from external innovation experts and a session with short presentations of the 10 finalist ideas. The Idébørsen at The Company was thus a whole concept including components as strategically defined themes for online organizational brainstorming, evaluation criteria, and roll out plan including deadlines, log ins, marketing in the internal newsletter and the company intranet, and information screens running commercials about the Idébørsen.

4   Analysis and Results

In this section we show the cultural dimensions that the respondents perceive are getting affected by the implementation of Idébørsen in the company. These dimensions summarized in table 5.

Table 5. Dimensions of Organizational Culture affected by IdeBørsen

Dimension	Idebørsen's contribution
Innovation awareness	Not streamline ideas (Atypical) are welcome Every employee can be a potential contributor A simple, low commitment, open and informal way to contribute ideas combined with a transparent and strategically based innovation process
Increased internal process orientation	Help moving from innovation anchored in consulting projects to employee-driven innovation, thus emphasizing internal process orientation in addition to customer process orientation
Empowerment and autonomy in decision-making	Help balancing broader bottom-up employee involvement and top-down strategic focus Opening up for empowerment, for example through the rating feature; however keeping final decision making with top management to ensure implementation.
Extrinsic and intrinsic reward orientation	The extrinsic rewards (the prizes given) are symbolic in nature and create visibility among peers. Intrinsic rewards are increased visibility and exposure within the company as well the potential of winning the idea competition contest and having the winning idea implemented.
Team working and knowledge sharing	Collaboration in Idébørsen – contributing to the development of other employees' ideas Insight into the knowledge of other colleagues – improving employees' ability to locate knowledgeable colleagues for potential collaboration
Integration and lateral interdependence and top management contact	Shortcutting the hierarchy in the innovation process (new roles of employees) Friendly competition Collaborating across departments Extended network to other organizational units or department

4.1   Innovation Awareness

Based on our case analysis, we find that the implementation of Idébørsen contributed to a different innovation awareness at The Company, encouraging "out of the box" thinking and a focus on innovations that are not solely tied to specific consulting projects. Idébørsen can thus be viewed as a complementary element that allowed for new types of ideas to emerge, thus changing the innovation practice, as clearly illustrated by one respondent:

"The Idebørsen can never substitute general internal development but it can support an innovation culture. (..) It is just the top of the iceberg. "Idébørsen" is not the solution to innovation in the organization as such, but it is a way to lift it [innovation] and make it more visible, which it is very strong at." Project manager (no.18)

In addition Idebørsen emphasizes new roles and tasks as well as a more open and informal approach to submission of ideas for innovation. It thus represented a break with the previous approach to innovation processes, which were related to specific projects and often hierarchically-driven. Many interviewees pointed out that Idebørsen encouraged a more widespread innovative behavior:

"Well it is putting innovation on the agenda in The Company and changing the innovation culture in The Company through a more innovative behavior" Idébørsen team (no.10)

"It motivates people to think about ideas" Project member (no.15)

Employees were rewarded for different roles: the owner of the best idea, the best commentator and the best stock exchange dealer. This was a way to engage more people in the process and create awareness about different tasks in the innovation process.

"It is not necessarily the one who needs and gets this idea who is most innovative. It may also be the one besides saying hey what if you do this, or it could be the set-up." Idébørsen team member (no.10)

In addition, Idébørsen made clear to employees that even ideas that at first seem irrelevant may end up having great value. Idébørsen emphasizes that innovative ideas may come from everybody and recognizes that innovation is not only about coming up with good ideas but also helping to develop others' ideas. It is a way to put innovation on the employees' agenda encouraging them to think in new ways, and inspire each other.

The idea format of Idébørsen provides an informal and non-demanding structure which made it easy for all employees to participate; however, the most important aspects are probably the transparency and the strategic anchoring of the process, which really communicate openness and sincerity about seeing all employees as potential innovation ideas contributors.

4.2   Increased Internal Process Orientation

Traditionally, innovation in The Company was developed and anchored in consulting projects, thus characterizing The Company as mainly having a customer orientation approach to innovation.

Disseminating the new ideas or innovations developed in the context of specific projects to the rest of the organization has always been difficult in the Company and primarily done through a tacit knowledge transfer process when employees participate and collaborate to different projects. However Idébørsen has opened up an internal process orientation by providing a platform for submissions of ideas from all employees, especially ideas which previously had no place to get aired or could quickly be stopped by the closest manager. Idébørsen has the potential to make The Company move towards a new balance, which values and requests not only a customer orientation but also an internal process orientation to innovation.

4.3   Empowerment and Autonomy in Decision-Making

The Company is characterized by many hierarchical decision making structures. Idébørsen, however, provides new elements for employees' empowerment and autonomy in decision making in relation to innovation both from the way the crowdsourcing process is organized and the way it functions.

From an organizational point of view, the set up and use of Idébørsen involved a high level of employee autonomy. The innovation manager established a team in charge of the enterprise crowdsourcing process comprising 8 employees from non-managerial positions. These employees represented different areas of expertise and different company locations, creating a sense of ownership of the crowdsourcing process across the organization. This team, which reported directly to the innovation director, developed and planned the crowdsourcing concept.

One of the team's decisions was to involve employees at all levels of the hierarchy through the different Idebørsen's roles: provider of ideas, idea commentator or idea "trader"   by buying and selling fictive shares, thus having the power to influence the ranking of ideas. This empowerment is clearly illustrated below:

"It is the employees, who enter and adjust it - why they believe some ideas are good or bad. It's been a game and they have had fun. Everybody can read about the ideas and comment whether they find it good or bad." Idébørsen team member (no.11)

4.4   Extrinsic and Intrinsic Reward Orientation

The set up and the reward structure of Idébørsen creates a way for not only rewarding the innovation champions, but also rewarding employees taking on different roles in the innovation process as already mentioned. The rewards are both extrinsic and intrinsic. The extrinsic rewards included the IPad given to the winner of the best idea. However, the most important were the intrinsic rewards such as gaining visibility in the organization, getting feedback on their ideas as well as the possibility of getting the winning idea on the strategic plan as the following statements shows:

"The best ideas would be taken into the strategy process, this was the real carrot you could say, that the ones who really came up as good ones, well they would be taken further" Idébørsen team member (no.10)

Idébørsen thus functions as an equalizer across all levels of the hierarchy by providing both explicit and intrinsic rewards.

4.5   Team Working and Knowledge Sharing

Idébørsen supports team working in multiple ways. First the technological affordances support team-work in an informal way, primarily by giving users the opportunity to comment on and rate others' ideas. Secondly, the allocation of a small group of experts to help the contributors of the selected ideas to further develop them creates an opportunity of formal team working.

In addition, Idebørsen has become a knowledge-sharing platform where the company employees can find inspiration for new ideas, learn how to go about working differently, find peers to work with, thus stimulating interaction and teamwork outside of the platform within and across the company's departments.

"It really is a tool for knowledge sharing. There is one who has found out an effective way to control drawings. We have talked about it... (No.18)

4.6   Integration, Lateral Interdependence and Top Management Contact

In The Company, the departments are the primary organizational units, even though a lot of projects involve cross-departmental teams, thus supporting collaboration across the organization as well as with customers and external partners. However, as noted earlier, a big challenge is the dissemination of project-based innovations to the rest of the organization. One advantage of Idébørsen is its ability to make ideas developed locally in an organizational unit visible to the rest of the organization, putting employees from different department in contact with each other in relation to specific ideas, thus supporting integration and lateral interdependence, while still maintaining the competitive spirit of each employee and department. This is done by establishing a kind of "friendly competition", with new types of social relations emerging between departments and individuals within the same department as the following shows:

"..One of the ideas I developed, I consulted a colleague. (..) I went up and asked one of the very experienced project managers: 'what do you do'." Project manager (no.18)

Lateral communication is enhanced and made easier in Idébørsen since contact formalities like status, function and work area are not needed. People only use their name, signaling therefore that all ideas are equally important.

"The advantage in this [Idébørsen] is the short between high and low in the system, so that ideas that may not get to the managers corridors they might get up there." Project member (no.14)

5   Discussion

By looking at the cultural dimensions in table 5 affected by Ideborsen, it can be concluded that the implementation of the crowdsourcing platform has brought about some changes in the organization that might show the beginning of an innovation culture change. Some of the results are directly linked to the innovation process and ideas generated; others are related to a more general agenda of increased collaboration and empowerment thus allowing the formation of new relations and access to new knowledge for the employees.

Importantly, Idebørsen gives employees the possibility to raise their voice and listen to colleagues' voices through a common platform that functions as an equalizer. Idebørsen breaks with the traditional project-related innovation processes that characterize the Company. Furthermore, by making participation in the process easier and more transparent, Idebørsen helps to overcome barriers to innovation imposed by organizational hierarchy.

Given the fact that the Company's employees are mostly engineers, Idebørsen's focus on valuable ideas that can be easily implemented is quite aligned with the way of working at The Company. Therefore Idebørsen supplements other fora of innovation in the organization such as the consulting projects in line with the findings from the Innovation Jams in IBM [7].

Value is created in a number of ways: it is fun, it creates a sense of community, it provides access to valuable knowledge, it provides visibility and status in the organization, and idea owners and commentators get direct feedback in the system. Likewise, the employees trust the system as they can see what is in there, the rules are clear and equal for everybody and the outcome is taken seriously. The potential to involve the majority of the employees and making the innovation process transparent has helped to create a whole new approach to innovation. Our case supports the notion that enterprise crowdsourcing, if implemented appropriately, can become a driver for change in the innovation culture, where participation in the innovation process becomes easier, more legal and more engaging. We thus concur with the argument of Doherty and Perry [10], who argues that a particular system may help reinforce particular values or may facilitate a change in the organizational culture. Our case does not suggest that the technology controls the innovation culture, but that it is a part of a techno-change system that can facilitate change [20]. In the case of Idébørsen we find that the current culture of innovation is challenged as more employees are invited to participate and new methods and new roles are established thus building up new relations.

6   Conclusion and Future Research

This study provides evidence that an organization may use an enterprise crowdsourcing system to make small changes in the organization innovation culture. The analysis shows that as a result of the crowdsourcing initiative, the Company has succeeded in putting innovation on the organizational agenda as an effort in which every employee has the potential to contribute in a number of different ways; as idea generator, idea developer, and idea commentator thus creating roles for everybody. In addition, the initiative complements the current customer orientation by enabling an internal process orientation towards innovation as also argued by [16] that is possible to do.   Finally, the crowdsourcing initiative supports knowledge exchange and collaboration across the organization by creating an opportunity to discuss ideas both in Idebørsen as well as in face-to-face social networks, supporting transparency of the process. It may thus be argued that Idebørsen reduces the organizational hierarchy and the internal borders. At the same time, Idebørsen has both supported and challenged the organizational culture. This is especially seen in the balance of empowerment versus management control and external versus internal process orientation.

This study is not free of limitations. For example, the number of the respondents is relatively small in relation to the total number of employees that have accessed or have potential access to Idebørsen. However the level of theoretical saturation found in our data justifies both the generalization from data to empirical description (level 1 inference) as well as the generalization from description to organizational culture theory (level 2 inference, [27]) in the context of our specific case. Further research could for example try to confirm the findings of this study in the context of other company settings, in an attempt for example to reach generalizing from theory to descriptions of other settings. It could be expected that future research investigating other organizations and their experiences with enterprise crowdsourcing could both find a replication of this study results as well as provide a more nuanced picture of its possibilities and limitations in influencing the innovation culture of an organization.

Nevertheless, our findings suggest that there can be organizational culture effects that follow the use of enterprise crowdsourcing, even though in our case company nothing can be said regarding whether these changes will continue to exist if and when Idebørsen will not be used anymore in the company.

References

1. Malone, T.W., Laubacher, R., Dellarocas, C.: The Collective Intelligence Genome. MIT Sloan Management Review 51(3), 21–31 (2010)
2. Brabham, D.: Moving the crowd at Threadless. Information, Communication, and Society 13(8), 1122–1145 (2010)
3. Lakhani, K.R., Kanji, Z.: Threadless: The Business of Community, Harvard Business School Multimedia/Video Case, pp. 608–707 (2008)
4. Huston, L., Sakkab, N.: Connect and Develop. Inside Procter & Gamble's new model for innovation Harvard Business Review, pp. 1–7 (March 2006)
5. Lakhani, K.R.: InnoCentive.com. Harvard Business School Case Study 9-608-170 (2008)
6. Vukovic, M., Lopez, M., Laredo, J.: PeopleCloud for the Globally Integrated Enterprise. In: Dan, A., Gittler, F., Toumani, F., et al. (eds.) ICSOC/ServiceWave 2009. LNCS, vol. 6275, pp. 109–114. Springer, Heidelberg (2010)
7. Bjelland, O.M., Wood, R.C.: An Inside View of IBM's Innovation Jam. MIT Sloan Management Review 50, 32–40 (2008)
8. Leidner, D., Kayworth, T.: A Review of Culture in Information Systems Research: Towards a Theory of IT-Culture Conflict. MIS Quarterly, 357–399 (2006)
9. Doherty, N.F., Doig, G.: An Analysis of the Anticipated Cultural Impacts of the Implementation of Data Warehouses. IEEE Transactions on Engineering Management 50(1), 78–88 (2003)
10. Doherty, N.F., Perry, I.: The Cultural Impact of Workflow Management Systems in the Financial Services Sector. The Services Industry Journal 21(4), 147–166 (2001)
11. Pliskin, N., Romm, T., Lee, A.S., Weber, Y.: Presumed Versus Actual Organizational Culture: Managerial Implications for Implementation of Information Systems. The Computer Journal 36(2), 143–152 (1993)
12. Hofstede, G.: Cultures and Organizations: Software of the Mind. McGraw-Hill, New York (1997)
13. Schein, E.H.: Organizational culture and leadership. Jossey-Bass, San Francisco (1985)

14. Wilkins, A.L., Ouchi, W.G.: Efficient Cultures: Exploring the Relationship Between Culture and Organizational Performance. Administrative Science Quarterly 28(3) (1983)
15. Tellis, J., Prabhu, C., Chandy, R.K.: Radical Innovation Across Nations: The Preeminence of Corporate Culture. Journal of Marketing 73(1), 3–23 (2010)
16. Denison, D.R.: Corporate culture and organizational effectiveness. John Wiley & Sons (1990)
17. O'Rielly, C., Caldwell: People and organizational culture: A profile comparison approach to assessing person-organization fit. Academy of Management Journal 34, 487–516 (1991)
18. Cameron, K.S., Quinn, R.E.: Diagnosing and Changing Organizational Culture: Based on the Competing Values Framework. Prentice Hall (1999)
19. Leavy, B.: A leader's guide to creating an innovation culture. Strategy & Leadership 33(4), 38–45 (2005)
20. Markus, M.L.: Technochange management: using IT to drive organizational change. Journal of Information Technology 19(1), 4–20 (2004)
21. Surowiecki, J.: The Wisdom of Crowds. Doubleday, New York (2004)
22. Hutter, K., Hautz, J., Füller, J., Mueller, J., Matzler, K.: Communitition: The Tension between Competition and Collaboration in Community-Based Design Contests. Creativity and Management 20(1), 3–21 (2011)
23. Andriole, S.J.: Business Impact of Web 2.0 Technologies. Communications of the ACM 53(12), 68–79 (2010)
24. Boudreau, K., Lacetera, N., Lakhani, N.: The Effects of Increasing Competition and Uncertainty on Incentives and Extreme-Value Outcomes in Innovation Contests. Management Science (2011)
25. Vukovic, M.: Crowdsourcing for enterprises. In: World Conference Services-I, pp. 686–692. IEEE (2009)
26. Pisano, G.: Profiting from innovation and the intellectual property revolution. Research Policy 35(8), 1122–1130 (2006)
27. Yin, R.K.: Case Study Research: Design and Methods. Sage Publications (1994)
28. Walsham, G.: Interpretive case studies in IS research: nature and method. European Journal of Information Systems (4), 74-81 (1995)

Electronic Communication between Citizens and Healthcare Practitioners: An Analysis of Practitioner Reported Obstacles

Polyxeni Vassilakopoulou and Miria Grisot

University of Oslo, Postboks 1080 Blindern, 0316, Oslo, Norway
{xvasil,miriag}@ifi.uio.no

Abstract. In this paper we document and analyze experiences and perspectives of Norwegian healthcare practitioners on citizen-oriented, electronic services. The electronic services include: booking appointments, renewing prescriptions, contacting healthcare providers, and getting e-consultations. Our study is based on the analysis of responses to a survey addressed to General Practitioner offices throughout Norway. We analyzed free-text responses from 156 doctors and 109 secretarial staff that already offer electronic services. The analytical framework for our study is based on the normalization process model (NPM) which focuses on factors that promote or inhibit routine embedding of technological interventions in existing work settings. The analysis reveals that the obstacles reported by healthcare practitioners relate mostly to exogenous (organizing) factors and workability (associated to the overall affordances of the technology implemented: asynchronous, text-based) and not to the specificities of the applications in place.

Keywords: Healthcare, Citizen-Provider Interaction, Web-based platforms, Normalization Process Model, Technologies-in-practice.

1   Introduction

Back in 2001, the Committee on the Quality of Health Care in America, issued the "Crossing the Quality Chasm" report where it identified the use of email and internet based communications as a way of meeting patients' needs more responsively and at a lower overall cost [1]. On a more general level, expanding the available means for interaction between citizens and healthcare providers, strengthening citizens' participation in the management of their own health and disease and encouraging a more proactive role is expected to result in more effective and efficient healthcare systems [2]. Furthermore, both the general public and healthcare providers express positive attitudes towards web-enabled interactions [3, 4, 5]. So, leveraging electronic communication means to offer new interaction possibilities within healthcare is viewed largely as desirable from a political, institutional and users' point of view.

Numerous web-based solutions for citizen-healthcare provider communication have been developed during the last decade but despite the expressed interest and positive stances, usage remains low [4, 6]. Research in the field of medical

T.H. Commisso et al. (Eds.): SCIS 2014, LNBIP 186, pp. 121–132, 2014.

informatics has identified several reasons for this slow uptake: lack of patients' and providers' education on the appropriate use of the technology [7], concerns of security and confidentiality [8], fear of heavy initial workload [9]. These concerns show that the adoption of technologies as email and internet for healthcare communication is not straightforward and that it entails a complex process in which relationships need to be renegotiated and reconstituted.

In Norway the government has recently released directives to grant citizens quick access to secure digital services. Following these directives the existing healthcare information infrastructure is expanding by putting in place a new, secure and reliable web based platform to facilitate citizen initiated communication with GP offices. However, a number of solution for digital communication are already implemented and in use in GP offices. Thus before the national solution is implemented is important to understand the current experience of those who are already users. Research within the field of Information Systems has shown that it is important not to study the potentiality of technological artifacts alone, but how this potentiality can get realized by embedding new technological artifacts in pre-existing sociotechnical arrangements [10, 11, 12].

The purpose of this study is to examine the experiences of General Practitioners (GPs) and medical secretaries that have already adopted web-based communications and to develop insights into the issues that they indicate as impediments for the introduction of web-based communication in their everyday work. The underlying assumption for this paper is that what matters for regular and wide-spread appropriation is not only technologies per se and their designed functionalities, but also, the bearing of specific technologies-in-practice (experienced technologies within their overall context) [10, 11]. Therefore, it is important to study the stances of those that have already been engaged with the particular technologies in their natural settings (healthcare professionals that have already experienced web-based interactions with citizens). The responses from this group of actual users can help us gain insight to situated and emergent issues that could not be captured by focusing to the details of the specific technological implementation (the specific new functionality offered). Therefore we address the following research question: what factors inhibit the assimilation of web-based communication in GP practices?

The paper is structured as follows. First, we present our case, and we describe the method used to collect and analyze our empirical data. Then we present our findings. Finally, we conclude by discussing insights from our analysis, pointing also to the limitations of our work and to possible directions for further research.

2   Case Background

The empirical material for our analysis is sourced from the study of the on-going Norwegian Government effort to put in place capabilities for simple and secure digital communication between citizens and primary healthcare providers. The aim is to make contact with health care services easier, and help citizens perceive the service as available and comprehensive [17]. The digital capabilities under study are part of a platform with a wider scope ("HealthNorway"). Apart from facilitating two-way communication between citizens and healthcare providers, the platform also hosts information (on prevention and treatments, patient's rights, and quality indicators for healthcare facilities), supports administrative e-services such as GP change and provides access to care record systems (starting with access to core medical records and active prescriptions). The development of the platform started in 2011 and "HealthNorway" has been already deployed while it is being continuously expanded.

What makes the case especially interesting is that the introduction of web-based communication between citizens and primary care has already been attempted through a number of private initiatives. Various vendors have developed modules for the Electronic Patient Record Systems (EPRs) that GP offices use or standalone solutions that allow digital communication with healthcare providers and booking of appointments over the internet. Private companies report that more than 65% of GP offices in Norway have adopted one of the commercially available solutions for web based communications (the first, second and third biggest providers report penetration in 45%, 12% and 10% of GP offices respectively) [18]. But although there is great availability of such solutions, less than 10% of the citizens use web based platforms to communicate with primary care healthcare providers for appointments, prescriptions, consultations or to cover their general information needs [18].

The government decided to include communication functionality in the national platform for three key reasons: a) to enhance uptake by improving outreach to the general public; b) to guarantee security (at a level that is only rarely provided by private solutions); b) to ensure ease of use for citizens (e.g. by providing many services in one place with a single login). Currently (spring 2014), there are ongoing activities for the syndication, design and development of the component that will support communication with primary care and a plan for piloting during autumn 2014.

3   Methods and Analytic Framework

3.1   Data Collection

The data collected cover both the mapping of the current situation for web-based citizen-primary healthcare communication in Norway and the stances of practitioners towards interaction mediated by digital capabilities. We have used available published data and we have also embarked to primary data collection. Table 1, summarizes our data sources and the type of information collected from each source. We verified the high penetration of web based solutions for the communication between citizens and GP offices by performing a survey that covered a 20% sample of all GP offices in Norway. Specifically, we applied a simple random sampling framework (equal probability of selection per office) to create our sample which contained 313 GP offices and then, checked the availability of web-based communication means for each office. We found that 73% of the GP offices had internet presence (a web site) and 76% of those offered digital communication services. This finding confirmed that availability did not result to significant uptake.

In order to explore factors that inhibit the assimilation of web-enabled interaction, we analyzed feedback that the Norwegian Health Directorate collected from GP offices (replies to a questionnaire distributed to all GP offices in the country). The feedback analyzed in this paper was collected in "free text" form. Practitioners were asked to report perceived disadvantages/issues of the use of web-enabled interaction.

We analyzed 265 completed answers received from 168 distinct GP offices that already have in place web-based communication services. The answers completed, returned and analyzed represent approximately 20% of the total GP offices that use web services in Norway. Out of the 265 completed answers, 156 correspond to GPs, while the remaining 109 correspond to secretarial staff. It should be noted that respondents did not only identify disadvantages but also emphasized the positive consequences of digital communication means. The analysis of perceived advantages is out of this paper's scope.

Table 1. Data Sources and Type of Information collected from each source

Data Source	Type of Information	Type of Analysis
Published Data	Citizens' use of GP office web solutions. GP offices' adoption of web solutions as reported by vendors.	Secondary analysis of data reported by the Norwegian Health Directorate.
Web Page Survey	Web presence and digital communication service offering of GP offices.	Primary data collection and analysis. Surveyed 20% of Norwegian GP offices (n=313).
GP office feedback on e-communication disadvantages	Factors that inhibit the "normalization" and routine use of the web-based communication	Content analysis of answers from 168 different GP offices.

3.2   Method for the Analysis of Feedback from GP Offices

The analytical framework for our study is based on the normalization process model (NPM)[19], which recognizes that in order to successfully introduce novel technologies in healthcare settings a "normalization process" that will rebalance technologies, people, practices, and values is required. We employed this model for analyzing the content of the feedback from the GP offices. NPM was developed for understanding the processes of implementing a complex intervention, and understanding how interventions become workable and integrated into everyday work [19]. It is a model grounded in sociology that aims to disentangle the collective action required for implementation [20, 21, 22]. The model focuses on factors that promote or inhibit routine embedding and, was derived from secondary analyses of multiple qualitative studies in health care settings.

There has been extensive use of the NPM to aid data analysis in systematic reviews of qualitative data [23]. The model includes four categories of factors for the routine embedding of complex healthcare interventions in service settings: interactional workability (IW), relational integration (RI), skill-set workability (SSW), and contextual integration (CI) [24, 25]. IW refers to the impact that a new technology or practice has on interactions, particularly the interactions between health professionals and patients (consultations); it captures *concerns related to disrupting the interaction between professionals and patients*. RI refers to the impact of the new technology or practice on relations between different groups of professionals, and the degree to which it promotes trust, accountability, and responsibility in inter-professional relationships; it captures *concerns related to undermining confidence in the knowledge and practice that underpins the interaction between patients and professionals.* SSW refers to the fit between the new technology and existing skill sets; it captures *concerns related to the fit with an actual set of roles or professional division of labor.* CI refers to the fit between the new technology and overall organizational context, including organizational goals, morale, leadership, and distribution of resources; it captures *concerns related to the integration within existing patterns of service organization and delivery.*

For every GP office response the two authors independently judged whether a statement relevant to the four NPM categories was present. Dual coding enabled differences in coding and interpretation to be identified and discussed [26]. In order to converge with our coding and stabilize our interpretations of the four categories of the model we had to go through more than five iterations. The use of a common coding framework helped us to single out specific issues and converge on them, but was very challenging to implement as the categories within NPM are ambiguously expressed and even seem to overlap [27]. In order to clarify the meaning of the categories we went through numerous papers where the NPM categories have been used for qualitative data analysis. Figure 1 presents the common coding scheme employed.

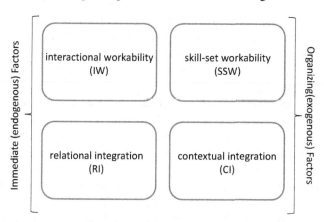

Fig. 1. NPM used as a coding scheme for content analysis of GP office responses

4   Findings

4.1   Overview of Findings

Our findings reveal a variety of issues raised by GP office personnel (doctors and medical secretaries). In figure 2 we provide some quotes from the responses.

Quotes from healthcare practitioners' responses

- "low threshold for contact, too many questions about trivialities"
- "patients write obscure messages on how urgently they need an appointment or what medications they order"
- "risk of sensitive data going astray"
- "losing control over the day"
- "some of the tasks are transferred from the medical secretary to doctors"
- "more work but less money, we also have the costs of this system without receiving any subsidy from the government for this."
- "pill addicts write long electronic messages "
- "patients are taught that healthcare is a shop , you book it - you get it. This is not healthcare, direct contact and examination remain important "
- "vulnerability to technical failure"
- "additional contacts to follow – this is added to electronic discharge summaries, e -link , e - prescription."

Fig. 2. Quotes from GP office personnel responses

Our analysis was intended to allow for a comparison of concerns across four different categories of factors: factors that relate to everyday task execution (workability both at the immediate and organizing level) and factors that relate to assimilation of novelty within the wider setting of healthcare (integration both at the immediate and organizing level).

Most respondents reported problems challenging the existing set of roles and professional division of labor. Problems of this type were coded under the skill-set workability category and include: increase complexity in everyday work as information from new channels need to be monitored and be acted upon, increase workload for doctors and less workload for support personnel (as citizens can now access doctors directly avoiding to go through the secretaries that have a gatekeeping role), loss of control over work hours as requests even for minor things can come during nights and weekends. Respondents also emphasized problems that result to disruptions in the interaction between healthcare professionals and patients. Problems of this type were coded under the interactional workability category and include: misunderstandings and uncertainty due to the limitations of the new communication modality (asynchronous, typed messages), distantiation/estrangement in the patient-provider relationship due to less frequent physical contact, procedural injustice (inability to offer novel services to needy patients that are not digitally literal e.g. older chronic patients that need prescription renewals). For contextual integration, health care providers emphasized issues related to challenges in the existing patters of service organization and delivery. These challenges included: absence of proper models for the reimbursement and the costing of services, privacy-security issues, issues related to the need to educate citizens in order to express their needs according to specific "service templates". Finally, within the relational integration category we classified issues related to undermining current professional knowledge and disrupting the interaction between professionals. This category includes problems related to the inability of secretarial personnel to assess the urgency for appointments with the limited information that citizens provide (which conveys a feeling of inadequacy), problems related to discrediting physical presence consultations (sending the message to patients that all healthcare needs can be catered for from a distance), problems related to limited availability of information to allow doctors assessing patient conditions holistically. Prominent themes emerging under each of the four NPM categories are shown in figure 3.

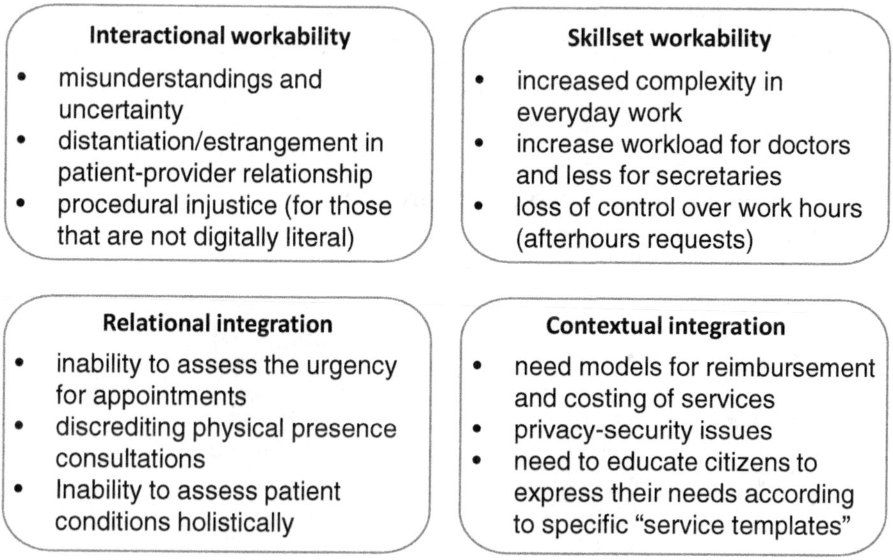

Interactional workability

- misunderstandings and uncertainty
- distantiation/estrangement in patient-provider relationship
- procedural injustice (for those that are not digitally literal)

Skillset workability

- increased complexity in everyday work
- increase workload for doctors and less for secretaries
- loss of control over work hours (afterhours requests)

Relational integration

- inability to assess the urgency for appointments
- discrediting physical presence consultations
- Inability to assess patient conditions holistically

Contextual integration

- need models for reimbursement and costing of services
- privacy-security issues
- need to educate citizens to express their needs according to specific "service templates"

Fig. 3. Prominent themes emerging under each of the four NPM categories

4.2   Differences across Groups

Variations across categories of factors and respondents' roles did exist (see figure 4). Nevertheless, the majority of concerns for both groups were related to workability (both at the immediate level, i.e. interactional and at the organizing level, i.e. skill-set related).

Overall, doctors have a stronger tendency to note disadvantages for the novel web-based communication means than secretaries (see figure 5). Although only half of the secretarial personnel identified specific disadvantages, more than two out of three doctors had a disadvantage to note.

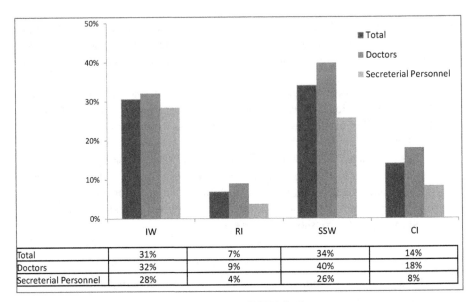

	IW	RI	SSW	CI
Total	31%	7%	34%	14%
Doctors	32%	9%	40%	18%
Secreterial Personnel	28%	4%	26%	8%

Fig. 4. Overview of NPM findings

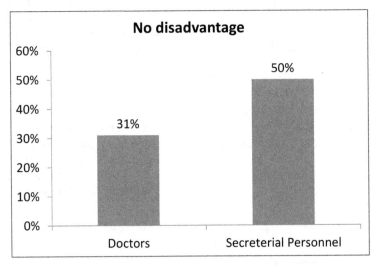

Fig. 5. Secretarial Personnel less critical than Doctors

There is a clear tendency among respondents to identify more issues related to everyday task execution (workability) rather than issues that relate to assimilation of novelty within the wider setting of healthcare (integration). Furthermore, doctors identified integration issues with a frequency which is more than double of the one of secretarial personnel (figure 6).

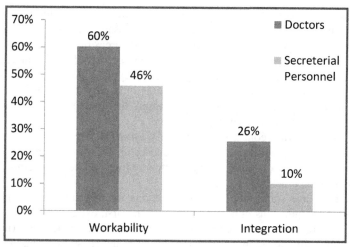

Fig. 6. Workability vs Integration issues identified by different categories of respondents

Although there was a very significant difference in the stances of doctors and secretarial personnel towards workability and integration, there was no such great difference among the two groups when comparing endogenous vs exogenous factors. (figure 7). Nevertheless, the tendency of doctors to identify more exogenous factors than secretaries is clear.

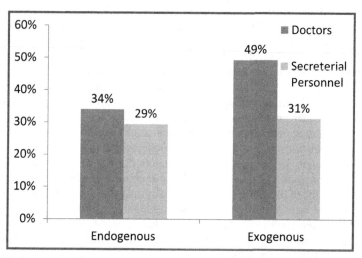

Fig. 7. Endogenous vs Exogenous issues identified by different categories of respondents

5   Discussion

Much of the literature about web based communication among citizens and healthcare providers has focused on specific functionalities/features and the overall citizen and practitioner perspectives about their use. Less attention has been placed on understanding the actual experiences of health care professionals and the issues they identify when reflecting on the impact of web-based communication means to healthcare provision. By avoiding to indicate specific areas of concern and predefined categories and allowing respondents to document perceived disadvantages freely, this study provided a unique opportunity to look beyond commonly reported issues (e.g. related to privacy concerns, communication ambiguity etc.). The data collected enable us to get insights on factors that inhibit the normalization of web-based communications in healthcare service provision.

We analyzed reported concerns qualitatively using NPM as a coding framework. This provided a conceptual framework that focuses on the work that needs to be done for a new technology or other complex intervention to become embedded and sustained in routine practice [25].

Our findings have some interesting implications for the successful embedding of novel communication means in healthcare provision. First, exogenous factors related to overall organizing seem to be even more prominent than endogenous (immediate) factors for the normalization of the technologies under study. This means that significant effort has to be made on issues that go far beyond the specific applications' functionality and interface design (e.g. an issue that has to be addressed relates to economic models for electronically mediated service reimbursement). Second, in order for health care professionals to adopt and use the electronic means effectively, workability has to be ensured. Workability is a concept that refers to the impact that the technology has on interactions between health professionals and patients and also refers to the fit between the technology and existing skill sets, actual sets of roles or professional division of labor. All these are very pragmatic everyday concerns expressed by practitioners. The findings suggest that NPM is a theoretical framework that facilitates understanding of experiences of health care work at the individual, as well as the organizational level. Although further exploration is necessary, our findings lay the foundation for orienting organized implementation efforts.

In a recent literature review [23] on the use of the normalization process framework it was identified that it has been employed successfully mostly to inform study/intervention design, to generate research questions for fieldwork, and to create tools for investigating and supporting implementation. But, it was noted that to fully explore the framework's full scope to shape implementation journeys, we need more studies that use it in a prospective manner during the planning stages of implementation projects to explore the real-world context in which the work will take place. In this extended literature review there was only one such study identified. Our research reported here aims to contribute to this type of NPM exploitation. By assessing the experiences of GP offices that already have some web-based communication means in place we can contribute to the better preparation for piloting the new national level web platform.

This study has several limitations. First, by design, it is the outcome of the analysis of responses of those that opted to give feedback to the Norwegian Health Directorate when asked for it. Although the overall sample (approximately 20% of the total) is significant, it is possible that it is not representative of the whole GP office population. It is possible that some categories of respondents are overrepresented and the whole data set is skewed toward some direction (e.g. towards practitioners that are more positively predisposed, or towards practitioners that have more free time than the average). Nevertheless, the input from such a big number of respondents is valuable and contributes important insights to the challenges of their everyday work.

Another limitation is related to the degree to which study participants have practical experiences with web-based communications. Given the limited citizens' adoption (less than 10% of the citizens use web based platforms to communicate with primary care healthcare providers in Norway [18]) it is probable that some GP offices that gave feedback did not have a real chance to get acquainted with the use of web-based technologies. Even with this constraint, however, we think that the contribution of all respondents is valuable for revealing inhibiting factors (stemming from rich or limited experiences).

Acknowledgments. The authors thank the professionals from the Norwegian Directorate of Health that supported this study. The views expressed in this paper are those of the authors and do not necessarily represent the views of the Directorate.

References

1. America IoMUCoQoHCi. Crossing the quality chasm: A new health system for the 21st century: National Academies Press (2001)
2. EU Council Decision. 2013/743/EU of 3 December 2013 establishing the specific programme implementing Horizon 2020 - the Framework Programme for Research and Innovation (2014-2020) and repealing Decisions 2006/971/EC, 2006/972/EC, 2006/973/EC, 2006/974/EC and 2006/975/EC. Official Journal of the European Union 2013 L347, 965-1041
3. Couchman, G.R., Forjuoh, S.N., Rascoe, T.G., Reis, M.D., Koehler, B., van Walsum, K.: E-mail communications in primary care: what are patients' expectations for specific test results? Int. J. Med. Inform. 74(1), 21–30 (2005)
4. Santana, S., Lausen, B., Bujnowska-Fedak, M., Chronaki, C., Kummervold, P.E., Rasmussen, J., Sorensen, T.: Online communication between doctors and patients in Europe: status and perspectives. Journal of medical Internet research 12(2) (2010)
5. Wakefield, D.S., Mehr, D., Keplinger, L., Canfield, S., Gopidi, R., Wakefield, B.J., Koopman, R.J., Belden, J.L., Kruse, R., Kochendorfer, K.M.: Issues and questions to consider in implementing secure electronic patient–provider web portal communications systems. Int. J. Med. Inform. 79(7), 469–477 (2010)
6. Spil, T.A., LeRouge, C., Trimmer, K., Wiggins, C.: Back to the future of IT adoption and evaluation in healthcare. International Journal of Healthcare Technology and Management 12(1), 85–109 (2011)
7. Moyer, C.A., Stern, D.T., Dobias, K.S., Cox, D.T., Katz, S.: Bridging the electronic divide: patient and provider perspectives on e-mail communication in primary care. The American Journal of Managed Care 8(5), 427–433 (2002)
8. Kittler, A.F., Carlson, G.L., Harris, C., Lippincott, M., Pizziferri, L., Volk, L.A., Jagannath, Y., Wald, J.S., Bates, D.: Primary care physician attitudes towards using a secure web-based portal designed to facilitate electronic communication with patients. Informatics in Primary Care 12(3), 129–138 (2004)
9. Mannan, R., Murphy, J., Jones, M.: Is primary care ready to embrace e-health? A qualitative study of staff in a London primary care trust. Informatics in Primary Care 14(2) (2006)

10. Orlikowski, W.J.: Using technology and constituting structures: A practice lens for studying technology in organizations. Organ Sci. 11(4), 404–428 (2000)

11. Feldman, M.S., Orlikowski, W.: Theorizing practice and practicing theory. Organ Sci. 22(5), 1240–1253 (2011)

12. Grisot, M., Vassilakopoulou, P.: Infrastructures in healthcare: The interplay between generativity and standardization. International Journal of Medical Informatics 82(5), e170–e179 (2013)

13. Star, S.L.: The ethnography of infrastructure. Am Behav. Sci. 43(3), 377–391 (1999)

14. Ribes, D., Finholt, T.A.: The Long Now of Technology Infrastructure: Articulating Tensions in Development. J. Assoc. Inf. Syst. 10(5), 375–398 (2009)

15. Hanseth, O., Lyytinen, K.: Design theory for dynamic complexity in information infrastructures: the case of building internet. J. Inf. Technol. 25(1), 1–19 (2010)

16. Eccles, M., Mittman, B.: Welcome to implementation science. Implementation Science 1(1), 1 (2006)

17. Norwegian Ministry of Health and Care Services. Stortingsmelding nr. 9: Én innbygger – én journal. Digitale tjenester i helse- og omsorgssektoren (2012)

18. Norwegian Health Directorate. Digital dialog mellom pasient og fastlege: nåsituasjon (2013), http://helsedirektoratet.no/it-helse/ehelse/fag-og-arkitekturutvalg/moter/Documents/Dagsorden.pdf

19. May, C., Finch, T., Mair, F., Ballini, L., Dowrick, C., Eccles, M., Gask, L., MacFarlane, A., Murray, E., Rapley, T., Rogers, A., Treweek, S., Wallace, P., Anderson, G., Burns, J., Heaven, B.: Understanding the implementation of complex interventions in health care: the normalization process model. BMC Health Services Research 7, 148 (2007)

20. May, C., Finch, T.: Implementing, embedding, and integrating practices: an outline of normalization process theory. Sociology 43(3), 535–554 (2009)

21. May, C.: A rational model for assessing and evaluating complex interventions in health care. BMC Health Services Research 6(1), 86 (2006)

22. May, C.: Towards a general theory of implementation. Implementation Science 8(1), 18 (2013)

23. McEvoy, R., Ballini, L., Maltoni, S., O'Donnell, C., Mair, F., MacFarlane, A.: A qualitative systematic review of studies using the normalization process theory to research implementation processes. Implementation Science 9(1), 2 (2014)

24. May, C., Mair, F., Finch, T., MacFarlane, A., Dowrick, C., Treweek, S., Rapley, T., Ballini, L., Ong, B., Rogers, A.: Development of a theory of implementation and integration: Normalization Process Theory. Implement Sci. 4(29), 29 (2009)

25. Murray, E., Burns, J., May, C., Finch, T., O'Donnell, C., Wallace, P., Mair, F.: Why is it difficult to implement e-health initiatives? A qualitative study. Implementation Science 6(1), 6 (2011)

26. Mair, F., May, C., O'Donnell, C., Finch, T., Sullivan, F., Murray, E.: Factors that promote or inhibit the implementation of e-health systems: an explanatory systematic review. Bulletin of the World Health Organization 90(5), 357–364 (2012)

27. Atkins, S., Lewin, S., Ringsberg, K., Thorson: Provider experiences of the implementation of a new tuberculosis treatment programme: A qualitative study using the normalisation process model. BMC Health Services Research 11(1), 275 (2011)

28. Hardiker, N.R., Grant, M.J.: Factors that influence public engagement with eHealth: a literature review. Int. J. Med. Inform. 80(1), 1–12 (2011)

29. Finch, T., Mair, F., O'Donnell, C., Murray, E., May, C.: From theory to'measurement'in complex interventions: Methodological lessons from the development of an e-health normalisation instrument. BMC Medical Research Methodology 12(1), 69 (2012)

Author Index